What She Didn't Tell You

· · · · ·

Pamela Hardy-Shepard Ph.D.

Jean Shepard Publishing, LLC

Library of Congress has cataloged first edition as follows:
Strong, Maria.
What She Didn't Tell You/Pamela Hardy-Shepard
1. Women-Self. 2. Women-Psychology. 3. Self-realization.

ISBN: 978-1-73506-200-6

This book is dedicated to all women.

It is my hope that this book empowers your life.

Remember: Lift as you climb.

CONTENTS

Preface

For more than thirty years of my life on this earth, I have mentored, coached, educated, and supported women on their life's journey. With each journey, I gleaned something new from each encounter. I began to wonder why some women's lives appeared to be blessed, whereas other women's lives were filled with disappointment and despair. Twenty years ago, I started a women's group called The Inside-Out Makeover. Once a month, women would get together to discuss self-help books, resources, and relationships. The name Inside-Out stuck because change begins first on the inside, with the residual changes eventually appearing outside. It is my aim with this book to encourage an inside-out transformation and the pursuit of your happiness.

I have always been a curious person, asking questions and having a need to sort out the answers. I spent two and a half years asking women from various backgrounds about their lives. I interviewed women on a one-on-one basis, hosted a Sip & Gab event (where women came together in a group), and conducted a survey to capture additional information on how women navigate their lives today. This book will look at the past and present lives of women who have elegantly leaned into their forty-fifth birthday and beyond. These women were selected because of their life's experience and insight, and the hope that comes from wisdom.

The women who were interviewed vary in their experience, education, and marital status. Each woman openly provided discernment coupled with brutal honesty. Collectively, these women share their experience of being a woman: growing into womanhood, what it is like to be married or single, keeping or losing friendships, and ideas on spiritual health and maturity. Their truthfulness is profound and rich in advice for women living and loving in the 21st century.

Introduction

Researching and writing this book made me realize that women have an enormous amount of power. Some women have power in the world, whereas other women maintain they have to have power in the bedroom. What do these women know that the rest of us women do not know? Reflecting, I realized I never thought about what it meant to have power either way. Power in the world or power in the bedroom? If I had to choose one, I would choose power in the world.

However, no matter which one a woman chooses, she will always have power, whether she realizes it or not. During the interviews, I asked women their thoughts, and as you will see, I received a myriad of responses.

Thinking about powerful women, Oprah Winfrey comes to mind. To me, power as a woman is the ability to make a mark in this world right where one stands and unapologetically display ones power through knowledge, skills, and faith. When I lived in Scotland, the most powerful woman in the world was Margaret Thatcher, the first female Prime Minister of Great Britain. She articulated with such confidence and was known for her stern demeanor. During her office time, she instituted a plethora of free-market reform while cultivating relationships with international leaders such as U.S. President Ronald Reagan and the Russian leader Mikhail Gorbachev. Women like Thatcher and Winfrey are powerful in their own right.

As you read each chapter, I ask you to consider your takeaway from each woman presented in this book. How did each woman use her power, talent, and skills to change the world from where she stood? I challenge each of you to think of the power you possess, the experiences you have encountered, and how you triumphed. I want you to remember when you were not always where you are today, and to please pass on your knowledge to others.

Chapter 1: I Am Woman

Where there is a woman, there is magic, and
her magic fills the air with roses of thought and
sunbeam of spoken word, unafraid of the power of
the gold between her legs and her dove like spirit.
—Pamela Hardy-Shepard

According to Merriam-Webster's Dictionary, a woman is an adult female person: a woman belonging to a particular category (as by birth, residence, membership, or occupation). After giving great thought about what a woman is, I realized it is difficult to capture the definition in one sentence. My mother gave me my first real glimpse of what a woman is, and her actions shaped me. I didn't realize it as a young girl, but as I matured, I realized that I learned what it means to be a woman by observing her behavior. My mother made sacrifices to ensure that her children had the best she could provide. She taught my siblings and me to nurture family, friends, and strangers. She provided great wisdom about life's trials and triumphs, with a backdrop of putting ourselves last. She taught vicariously by doing and not saying. She worked hard to provide for her children. There was not one time during my childhood, my teen years, or my young adulthood when I saw my mother purchase anything for herself or do anything significant for herself. Raising my own family, I did the same. I put myself last. When I went shopping, I would purchase something for everyone else but myself. Without any thought on what was driving this in me, I never considered buying myself anything. In retrospect, I thought that was what made a good mother. And unfortunately, without even knowing it, I taught my two daughters to do the same thing.

Not only did I watch my mother's behavior, but I also watched the behaviors of the women in my neighborhood. The women in my neighborhood did not have a problem showing their thoughts—positive or negative.

Reflecting, I now can see that most of the women I knew were unhappy. I never saw them smile or have a kind word for children. I watched the women in my neighborhood who were always too good to even look in one's direction. As a child (and still now), I was not too fond of these women. I never wanted to be like them: judging others and speaking in a condescending tone, as if the person they were speaking to did not notice.

A life-changing event occurred when I traveled to Jamaica. I attended a conference called Sisters Jammin, and I met author Debrena Jackson-Gandy. Debrena taught the women at the conference how to say no and mean it without guilt or shame. She taught us to say no when someone wanted to add another project, meeting, or volunteer opportunity to an already filled plate. She said, "Tell whoever is asking for your time, 'That does not work for me.'"

After the conference, I returned home, all fired up to exclaim my NO on the world. I got my first opportunity at my job, where I was asked to add another meeting to an already full schedule. I calmly replied, "Thank you for the invite; however, the meeting does not work for me." I felt my hair on the back of my neck stand up! I was emboldened to do it again; I found another source of power I didn't know existed.

Collectively, the women I observed growing up ultimately defined what a woman is to me. I see how my mother's wisdom and anecdotes for life helped me determine who I am as a woman, wife, mother, grandmother, and friend. I can also see how each woman in my neighborhood helped shape me. I took from each woman what I needed and discarded what I did not want or need. From the research I conducted, it is the same for many of the women in this book.

Each interview provides a glimpse into how diverse we are as women. When we were born, how we were raised, where we were raised, and by whom we were raised makes a difference. Each woman has a story to tell. As women, we wield a lot of power just with our presence. It is high time to own your power. Where there is a woman, there is magic! It is yours—OWN IT!

• • • • •

Angela, 58, single, mother, and grandmother

Some women have power in the world, whereas others claim they have it in the bedroom. What are your thoughts?

Hmmm… I never thought about us women like that… Power! Hmmm. I think I would take power in the world. It appears having power in the world is more important than having power in the bedroom; what would power in the bedroom get me? By having power in the world, I would have power in the bedroom as well!

What would having power in the world get you in the bedroom?

I believe I will learn to negotiate my needs better.

Could you explain a little more?

I would know how to communicate my needs effectively to my partner.

How will that encourage power in the bedroom?

Some people think of power in the traditional sense—Do what I say. Power to me is to use my words effectively and sweetly to get what I want and how I want it.

As a woman, where did you get your sense of who you are and who you will become? From your mother? Father? Friends? Society?

I have never once thought about that question. I got a sense of who I am as a woman from my mother and grandmother. My mother did not talk to me about being a woman. I was not told about my period, or my breasts getting bigger, or how my body would continue to change. I was told to stay away from boys and not be 'fast' like the girl down the street.

How did you find out about your period?

I found out about my period in the most embarrassing way—at school! I was told by my arch enemy, Crystal Bates. She was one of the most popular girls at school, but I thought she was mean and unkind to other girls if they did not have nice clothes like her. Crystal told me, 'You have something on your pants; you better go to the nurse's office.' I ran to the nurse's office, and there was blood on the back of my favorite light-blue pants. I felt so embarrassed. The nurse called my mother, and she came to school and took me home. It was at that time that my mother decided to tell me what was going on with my body. As a child, I thought something was wrong with me, or I was dying. My mother assured me that I was not dying. Looking back, I feel that it could have been avoided. I finally got past the nightmare but thinking about it now makes me wonder why my mother did not tell me! Now that I am thinking back, Crystal Bates was mean to most girls; she did not have to say a word to me, but she directed me to go to the nurse's office. That was a nice thing she did!

On weekends, we went to my grandmother's house, and we would pick snap peas and greens from her garden. My mother and grandmother would wash the greens in the sink, adding salt to the water to take off the bugs, and they would talk forever. I would act like I did not hear what they were saying, but I would listen as they talked about church and what people were wearing or someone's hairstyle. Most of their conversations were around sales at the grocery store, someone's child acting up, and the plans for our family reunion. My mother and grandmother taught me to cook, clean, and to be respectful.

How would you describe your relationship with your mother?

When I was a little girl, my relationship with my mother was normal. We talked and laughed a lot. My mother would help me with my homework; she would help me pick clothes out for school and for church.

Now that you ask me, it seemed like the older I got, the less we really talked to each other. I knew the rules and did not go outside of the rules. If we went shopping for clothes, she never liked any of the outfits I selected.

That is certainly normal for most mothers!

My mom bragged to her friends about me as if I was not standing there.

How did that make you feel?

I felt fine. She never said a negative thing about me. But the older I got, I did not like her doing that, and I asked her to stop. My mother told me that she was proud of me! I said, 'Mom, why don't you tell *me* you are proud of me?' And my mother said, 'I do tell you.' It seemed after that, I felt our relationship began to change. I must say, I was not the sweetest daughter, either. I did things to irritate my mom, like chew with my mouth open, mix the white clothes with the dark clothes in the washing machine. I didn't always do what I was told to do, for instance, sweep the floor after dinner or pick my clothes up off the floor in my bedroom or be in when the streetlights went off. My mother would get frustrated because I wanted her to do things like my other friends and their mothers. My mother would say, 'I am your mother, I am not your friend. It is my responsibility to raise you and love you.'

What things did you wish your mother would have told you?

A lot of things! Are you ready for this one? I really wish my mother had told me that my pubic hair would turn gray!

I remember that day like it was yesterday. I was about to turn thirty years old, and I noticed a lot of gray hair down there. I must have not seen the first few gray hairs, but on that day, I saw several gray hairs, and the sight of long gray hair totally freaked me out! I literally got mad! I called my closest friend Beverly and asked her did she have gray pubic hair? Beverly laughed and said, 'Really?' She said it happens to us all. And then she began to tell me what others told her: Cut it off! Shave it off! Wax it off! Or dye it! Dying my hair down there was out! In the end, I cut it close and kept it off.

You know, this brings me to another thing. I wish my mother had told me that my cleavage between my breasts would begin to wrinkle one day, and my breasts would slap together like two children fighting under a blanket. I would have liked to have known the changes my body would go through as I matured. I am sure it is different for every woman. Maybe I would have done something different, but that is something I will never know. As we are having this conversation, looking back, my mother did not tell me about my period. Why would she tell me about other things about my womanhood or sexuality? Because of my experience, I do my best to tell young women to take care of their body, eat right, get enough sleep, watch who you hang around. I tell young girls and younger women to make sure their friends are positive and want to do something with their lives. The kind of friends that will support you, the kind of friends who will lift you up when you are down. The kind of friends who will support your ideas, and who will tell you the truth!

What else do you share with younger women?

I tell them to choose themselves first before you choose anyone else. Love yourself, every part of you! As women, we all have something about ourselves that we don't like. The media does not help, either. They show us flawless women with perfect bodies, hair, and makeup. I tell young girls that the models in the magazines have been airbrushed, they are not perfect. Love yourself for who you are! I share with young women that each woman brings an assortment of gifts and talents to the world; don't let anyone tell you differently.

> *Choose yourself before you choose anyone else.*
> *Powerful words to live by.*

• • • • •

Donna, 65, mother of two

As a woman, where did you get your sense of who you are and who you will become? From your mother? Father? Friends? Society?

Many people showed me what it is to be a woman. First, it was my mother and my father too! They both would talk to me, but differently and on different topics. My mother shared with me around eleven years old that I would become a young woman soon and really made it sound special. She explained the facts of life, and we talked about me getting my period. We would talk about spiritual matters, beauty, and keeping my body clean, like making sure I took a bath and kept my underwear clean. We would talk about getting involved with groups at school. My mother taught me how to cook and clean. My father would talk to me about how much he loved me, and the guy that gets my heart must treat me like a queen. My father would refer to how he treated my mother. I would see them kiss and hug each other. I would jokingly stick out my tongue like I was getting sick. But I knew they loved each other deeply. I would see my father come in the kitchen while my mother was cooking breakfast and walk up behind her and just hold my mother and kiss her ever so gently.

My father was a good man. He taught me to have a voice and stand up for what I think is right. He told me not to let anyone take advantage of me and that I am loved by him and my mother.

What a blessing to have a father such as yours.

You never know how much you have until it's gone. My father died seven years ago, and nothing has ever seemed the same. My mother seemed to lose her zest for life when my father died. She has not been the same ever since. My sisters and I do our best to convince her to enjoy her life. She does not want to talk about it. We are all hurting, especially during the holidays. My father loved Christmas, and he made us love it too! He would ask my sisters and me to spy and interrogate our mother to find the perfect gifts for her.

It sounds as though your parents had a wonderful life together. As a woman, what did you garner from seeing your two parents in a loving, committed relationship?

I know my parents did not wake up that way; it took work to have and keep a great relationship. My mother would tell us that we teach people how to treat us! In your relationship, you must communicate and fight fair. She taught us when having an argument with your spouse, stay on the topic and don't bring things into the argument from the past. We must argue to resolve and not to be right. My mom would add that you may be right in the situation, but you can be right and all alone. My mother would repeat over and over. 'Don't take everything personally when you need to speak about something.' She would say, 'Put it on you by using how you feel.' Finally, she said never accuse your husband of anything no matter how hard it is, and for heaven's sake, don't shut down. I did not take my mother's advice very often, and my ex-husband never heard of fighting fair. He thought fighting fair was being the loudest voice in the room. That's why he's my ex!

My mother also discussed things such as when people see a happy relationship. Instead of admiring a great marriage or relationship, my mom would say some women become jealous of your relationship. Don't be dismayed. Great relationships take work. She used to make me laugh when she would say, 'Men spend more time taking care of their cars, lawnmowers, and watching their sports team than they do invest in their relationships.' Women too! Women spend more time dieting, researching the latest hairstyles, fashion, or washer and dryer and shopping in general than working on their relationships. She also told us not to tell our relationship business to everyone. My mother taught us not to envy anyone. If you want something, go after it for yourself!

What are some of the things you wished your mother had told you?

I wish my mother had taught me how to say no! All my life, I have been saying yes to everyone, trying to make everyone else happy: my ex-husband, children, friends, and my job.

I'm exhausted all the time. I don't have an exciting weekend on the horizon. I have run myself into the ground, doing everything for everyone! I feel that I don't have a life. I watch my friends enjoy their weekends with their families and friends while I'm doing laundry, cleaning the house, getting my clothes ready for work, and running errands.

Is this by choice?

Not by choice, but by circumstance.

Would you like to explain a little more about your last comment? (Immediately, Donna said no, so I moved on to the next question.)

Do you have someone special in your life?

No, I do not have anyone.

Would you like to tell me more?

There is nothing to tell. I got divorced. I am older, and men stopped looking at me! They look at the twenty or thirty-something girl with the big full breasts and the little waistline. I have big breasts, but my waistline stopped being small when I turned forty-eight. I don't think I'm a bad-looking woman, but men don't see me; I am invisible.

I am a good woman. I am smart, I am good with money. I guess that does not count today.

I wanted to circle back, if you don't mind. You said, 'Men do not see me; I am invisible.' Could you explain a little more?

Yes, I can. It doesn't matter where I am—the grocery store, the mall, or a fast-food restaurant—men don't look at me. They look past me to other women who have more revealing clothes, fake lashes, and have a four-hundred-dollar bag on their arm. I cannot compete with that.

What men don't realize is that they will pay for all those things that they see. Lashes, purses, and salons are expensive. I don't judge other women who have them. I am not saying it is okay to look any old way, but all those things are not for me. Still, I know that there is someone for me!

You will have to get out more, because unfortunately, your future date does not know your address! (We both chuckled.) What do you do for fun? Do you go anywhere to meet others?

I want to go places, but I don't want to be a third wheel with my friends and their spouse or boyfriend.

Have you thought about a club or something you are interested in?

Like what?

Do you like to travel, attend plays, drink wine, dance, etc.?

I like to travel, and I like plays, but I never thought about joining a club. I'm going to check into the travel club! Thank you!

You are most welcome! If you were to give advice to younger women, what advice would you give?

Enjoy what you have! If you are beautiful, act that way on the outside! Be kind to others. Take great care of yourself, put yourself first if you can. Do not go through stop signs with men or your friends. Read more, take classes, get a hobby, and be grateful for where you are and what you have! Keep your heart and mind focused on God.

Some women believe they have power in the world, whereas other women maintain they have power in the bedroom. What are your thoughts?

I want power in the bedroom because that is where my power matters. Unless I own Amazon, Apple, or hold an office in government, my power would be minimal in the world.

Why minimal power?

What platform do I have? Who would listen to me?

What about the women in your circle? You have power and influence where you are! Tell me more about power in the bedroom.

Having power in the bedroom would mean that I would have the confidence in myself, my body, and my expression of my love. I would be able to strut my stuff and feel comfortable in my skin.

Do you have that now?

No, I am not there. After going through a divorce, I feel that I lost my confidence. Maybe that is why men don't see me, because I do not see myself!

What will it take to have this power return to your life?

I think I would have to accept my body for what it is. Not how I wish it would be, but how it is right now. For me, it is going to take baby steps! Taking one day at a time.

As I reflected on Donna's response to the power in the world or power in the bed, I began to wonder: How many other women do not know the power they wield?

How do you convey your power in the world?

• • • • •

Cari, 57, re-married, two children

(My interview with Cari took a while to get started. She seemed to be holding back.)

As a woman, where did you get your sense of who you are and who you will become? From your mother? Father? Friends? Society?

My mother.

Could you provide a little more information?

Absolutely not!

(I felt that I had offended Cari because she responded so abruptly.) Are you okay? We can stop now if you would like.

No, I would not like to stop. I now realize there were so many things that my mother did not tell my sister and me about relationships.

My mother told us how men were up to no good, how they cheat, how they spend money. What I now realize talking to you is that my mother never told my sister and me anything positive about having or keeping a relationship with the men in our lives. She never mentioned how a man should love me and how I should love him back!

Maybe my husband is not a dirty dog after all. I did not give him a chance to love me. I felt that he would do little underhanded things that proved my mother was right. I see it now; I repeated things from previous relationships and brought them to my current relationship. What I now believe is what I was getting all those years in relationship after relationship, I created by what I had been thinking and expecting. I thought it, I looked for it, and guess what? I always found what I was looking for: the worst in men!

How will you go forward from here?

I think I will start with my attitude. I need to work on myself and my issues.

Based on what we discussed here today, what advice would you give women regarding relationships?

First, they need to know who they are as a person. They need to figure out what they learned from their parents. Did they see love demonstrated in the home? Don't be like me, don't live your mother's nightmare. Learn about your strengths and gifts as a woman. What are you passionate about? Know that you have untapped greatness. Are you a writer, a dancer, a poet, an advocate, or an activist? You can be whatever your heart wants to be. Love yourself first! When you love yourself, you will not let anyone mistreat you! I have come to learn if you think men are dogs, the dogs will always bark at you. My mother had bad experiences with men. Therefore, she taught us not to trust men.

Talking about it now, I wish things had happened differently for my mother. I wish my mother could have used her experience differently. I think our mother was only trying to protect my sister and me from the hurt she experienced. One or two experiences do not make all men bad. I guess one would have to ask, what role did my mother play? Maybe because my mother only expected negative things in her life, negative things showed up. I wonder what would have happened if she thought more positively.

What would be your advice to younger women?

This is important, so please hear me! Do your best to stay away from women who think all men are dogs! Yes, some men deserve that category. Sure, there will be complaints from time to time in any relationship. If you are complaining about your boyfriend or husband, please get a mirror and look at yourself. The problem could be just you! Trust them unless they have given you a reason not to trust them. Please do not make them pay for the other guy's bad behavior. And women, stop looking in the garbage for good men. We teach people how to treat us. Treat yourself well, and others will do the same.

As I began to reflect on Cari's interview, her last two sentences resonated with me. 'Stop looking in the garbage for good men.' If we always do what we have always done, we will always get what we have always gotten!

*Do something different and expect a
different outcome!*

Chapter 2: A Voice in the Darkness

Each interview offers a glimpse into how diverse we are as women. When you were born, how you were raised, where you were raised, and who you were raised by makes a difference. Each woman has a story to tell. As women, we wield a lot of power just with our presence. Where there is a woman, there is magic! It is yours—own it!

For centuries, women's voices have been silenced to a whisper, despite the song inside them. Men have dominated the landscape, from business to love relationships. Women's voices matter! Collectively, we have formed a song of self-determination to speak our minds with pleasure and tenacity!

In this chapter, you will learn about the struggle, heartache, and the victories of women who have spoken up to be the voice in the darkness.

• • • • •

Nikki, 50, single, advocate, and personal coach

Hi, I'm Nikki. I am a little shy, but I want to share my story if it helps someone's life. I am one of six children. I am the third-born child of my parents,

Edmond and Betty. My parents were amazing. They gave us plenty of love and common sense. We grew up in a tight-knit community. We knew all our neighbors, unlike now. I don't know any of my neighbors. I was a tomboy who liked to be with the boys, fighting, racing soapbox derby cars and skateboarding. I was nothing like my sisters, who wanted to have tea parties and play with dolls. At first, it was okay that I played with boys—until I got older. Then it seemed all of a sudden I was expected to be interested in wearing dresses and acting feminine, something I had no clue.

As the years moved on, I felt like I was different. The boys that I used to play with acted as though I had cooties. The girls were into makeup, clothes, and boys. It was sickening to me. I realized that I did not fit in anywhere, so I mostly stayed to myself. I got excellent grades throughout junior high and high school. I grew up playing soccer and continued to play throughout high school.

I received a soccer scholarship and played all four years in college. In my junior year, I realized that I was attracted to women. I became involved with another player on the team. I had never been in a relationship with anyone, and I fell hard... and that is another story for another time.

On many occasions, I tried to tell my family about Mellie and me but did not know how. I now wish I had just told them and dealt with it then. Unfortunately, my family found out about me and my relationship from a neighbor whose son attended the same college. Our neighbor's son saw me kissing and holding hands with Mellie at a party.

When my parents found out I was gay, it did not hurt them about me being gay. It was the way they found out that I think hurt them the most. If I could change one thing, it would have been to tell my parents and family first.

Once my parents and siblings got over the shock, my family showed love and acceptance. If I had one piece of advice to give anyone, I would say first, be honest with yourself, and second, tell your truth whatever it is. Don't be ashamed of who you are! Share only with those individuals who matter in your life.

I am not saying that by telling your truth you will always have a happy ending. I have heard horror stories where some families disown the person who comes out and speaks their truth. Be proud of who you are, not who people think you are or want you to be. Because of my experience, I became an advocate and coach others who have come out to live their lives to the fullest.

What I garnered from Nikki's insight is we must first be truthful to ourselves above all others. My mother used to say, 'Old Father Time is a storyteller!' For me, I would rather be the one to tell my story.

What stories can Old Father Time tell about you?

• • • • •

Hope, 60, married, nurse practioner

I was a regular kid growing up. I wanted to be a teacher, nurse, and mailman, all at once. As a child, I thought everyone loved teachers and nurses because families gave them great gifts. I did not see the mailman get anything special. Although, every year at Christmas time, my mother would bake cookies for Mr. Sprig, the mailman. I didn't think his gifts were as good as the gifts that Mrs. O'Bryan, my second-grade teacher, received, so I decided to be a teacher or a nurse.

Thinking back, I had a great childhood. We would play outside all day, into the evening. My friends and I would go to the house for only three reasons: water, lunch, and a bathroom break. We stayed outside until our parents would say it was time to come in the house, unlike the kids of today who sit in the house glued to a TV or screen playing video games. As young kids, we had fun going to the county fair, swimming, camping, and sleepovers with friends.

Throughout my school years, I had lots of friends. I was a cheerleader and was continually active on the debate team. A month after I graduated from high school, I married my high school sweetheart. Shortly after, we had two kids, and I never lost the baby weight. I no longer had that cheerleader body. I tried everything from Jenny Craig to Weight Watchers to starving. I lost weight but was not able to keep the weight off. I would lose weight only to gain it all back with an additional ten or fifteen extra pounds. I would start a workout program only to quit halfway through the program because I was physically out of shape. Working out at the time was just too much for me. As things would have it, my husband and I started having problems. Problems that were already in the marriage. Our relationship began to disintegrate right before my eyes.

To make a long story short, we split up. I had full custody of the children, and I worked full-time to make ends meet. My job did not pay enough, and child support helped a little but did not make a difference. Two years later, I decided to go back to school to get my Master of Science in Nursing. Six months after graduation, I landed my dream job as a nurse practitioner. Life was looking up for the kids and me. I was purchasing a home with a big back yard for the kids and an extra room to create my long-awaited meditation/exercise room when I was diagnosed with cancer. I initially thought it was a joke; I did not believe it was right for almost a week. I was in denial, and I walked around in a daze.

The best part, if you can call it that, is the cancer was caught in enough time. The cells had not spread beyond the breast, which means I had a ninety-nine percent survival rate and that stage 1 is treatable. I opted for surgery but did not want radiation treatment. My mother came to stay to take care of the kids and me when she fell and broke her hip.

I wondered what else could go wrong. Since my mother was out of commission, the kids' father helped when he could. He had remarried and recently had a new baby. The kids did not want to stay with Lance and his wife because, in their hearts, the kids felt that Lance had deserted them ever since his son was born.

I did my best to convince them differently and just prayed that they would someday understand that their father loved them dearly. Fast forward one year later, I have a clean bill of health. I went back to work and finally bought that long-awaited house. We moved and got settled in, and I recognized that our lives had been in a constant state of an upheaval of some kind for the past five years. As things slowed down, I finally had time to look around at my life and breathe. I was certainly happy that there was less drama, but I felt something was missing.

For six months, I felt a weird feeling in the pit of my stomach. It was hard to explain, but it would not go away.

I remember this like it was yesterday. I was at work, and a well-dressed gentleman came up to me and introduced himself as Gregory Abbott. He said, 'You should be in movies.' I blew him off with a shrug and a laugh. He said, 'This is your time, and when you are ready to soar, give me a call.' He handed me his card and walked away. I read the card in my hand and turned to watch him disappear down the hall.

I thought to myself, how weird is this? I said to Kate, the other nurse at the nursing station, 'Did you see what just happened?'

Kate said, 'Of course I saw it. I was right here, and I think you need to call him.'

'He could be a freak; I am not calling him.'

'Well, I think you should call. It's just a call. You're not marrying the man. Look, just hear him out. If you feel threatened or your gut tells you this is wrong, end the call. You don't have to give him any information about you.'

I put the number in my jacket pocket and forgot about it until the next morning. Tuesday was wash day, and I started checking pockets and found the card. I stared at the card and later put it on the top of my dresser. One week later, I got curious and called the number. A woman answered the phone, 'Good morning, the Banner Agency, Kelsey speaking.'

I immediately got tongue-tied and didn't know what to say. I finally etched out some words, 'I was given this number by a man about a week ago.'

Kelsey replied, 'Yes, ma'am. I will transfer your call.'

I was thinking to myself, 'Where is she transferring my call to and to who? I never said my name.'

Within a few seconds, a male voice answered the phone.

'I was hoping you would call. My name is Gregory Abbott. I know this seems a little strange. I am sure nothing like this has happened to you before. Please hear me out, and then if you don't like what you hear, you can hang up. I am a talent agent, and it is my job to find talent. I am good at what I do. I know beauty and talent when I see it. When I saw you at the nursing station, I knew I had to reach out to you.'

An in-depth conversation ensued, and Mr. Abbott convinced me to come to Studio City and the Banner Agency. I searched the internet and found the agency; it seemed legitimate. Women's intuition told me to take another person with me.

I asked one of the male nurses if he could go with me to Los Angeles. Jason and I had to get our schedules together, and a week later, we drove to Los Angeles.

We arrived in Studio City. I had my interview, and everything moved so quickly after that meeting. I was driving to Los Angeles every other week filming commercials. I later became a stand-in for other actresses. I started doing commercials here and there. I saved enough money to take my kids on vacation to Europe. It was my vacation that changed my life for good. Five days into our vacation, we were in Rome, Italy. We had a tour scheduled to see the Colosseum, Sistine Chapel, and the Vatican Museum when our tour bus got a flat tire. We all filed off the bus looking for a place to eat or sit. The kids and I found a little place not too far from where the bus broke down that served banana bread and some expresso for me. Walking back to the bus, we met up with two other passengers from the bus.

A nice-looking man asked, 'Where did you get that scrumptious banana bread?'

I told him where to find the banana bread and continued walking. My daughter said, 'Mom, he likes you.'

I laughed and said, 'No, silly, he asked me about the banana bread.' My daughter told me that he was flirting with me. It is sad to say, I didn't even know it. Because of the bus's flat tire, we were unable to visit every tour. The tours we did attend, we were accompanied by Anthony, the nice-looking man, recently divorced like me, and his daughter Lizzie for the rest of the tour. Anthony and I stayed in touch for a year, talking on the phone and sending pictures mostly. About the second year of our friendship, we became exclusive, and we would visit each other for long weekends.

On year three, we started making plans for our future, and today, Anthony is now my husband

Wow, I did not see that coming. Congratulations! What have you gleaned from your experience that would provide hope for other women?

Life can be a mystery, it has twist and turns, but in the end, it brings you to a place where you want to be. I would tell myself that I will meet a man of my dreams one day, and I did. Every experience brought me to my life as it is today. Yes, terrible things happened, but I did not let those things keep me from visualizing the good! Where you are today is the residual of what you believe and what you have been thinking. Things will happen the way they are supposed to occur.

Change your mind and change your life.

• • • • •

Marcy, 49, single, business owner

Tell me a little about yourself and your journey.

I was an abused child. I hated my life growing up. The only time I felt good was when I was not at home, because my father beat our mother and us. I think everyone knew what was going on, but no one helped us.

Our house was like the action movie *King Kong vs. Godzilla*! There was always a fight or an argument that ended up in a knockout battle.

My little brother and I walked on eggshells to stay out of trouble. My father was an alcoholic, and when he drank, he was the ugliest person I knew. Because of his drinking and abuse, we mostly stayed in our bedrooms to stay out of his way. I would never invite anyone to our house. My dad would fly into a frenzy if there was not enough money to buy a bottle of Jack Daniels. He would blame my mother, thinking she was spending up the money.

Interestingly enough, he would always get a bottle of something or beer. Because of the fighting, the police were called regularly to our house, and my brother and I ended up in the foster care system at ten and twelve. The best part is that we were together, but we were moved from home to home.

Some of the foster parents and their children liked us, and the others liked the money more. Two years into foster care, my brother and I were separated. The separation was painful for us both because we were all we had.

After the separation, I felt like I was in prison, so I ran away three times from that home. The last time I ran away, I was placed into a new home. Ms. Catherine Bell was a nice woman who took several foster children into her home. When I arrived, I was angry and destructive to myself and those around me. I became a bully, though I only bullied those I thought were a threat to me. At school, I would take up for the bookworms or anyone I thought was like me.

I was protecting them from the taunts of the rich and popular kids and their little snobby cliques. In the school I attended, there was a division between the rich and the poor, the haves and the have-nots. These kids were mean, but they were mean in a way that the teachers and administration turned a blind eye. The teachers let them get away with things that the rest of us could not. I think they did this because of their parents' status. Every chance I could, I stood up for the little guy at school because I felt no one stood up for them.

When I moved in with Ms. Bell, that is when things started to change. I would get in fights and would get suspended. Ms. Bell would come to school and get me each time.

I remember her saying, 'When you change your thinking, your life will change.'

Her words stuck with me and still bring tears to my eyes today. When Ms. Bell would pick me up from school, she would always ask me, 'Are you alright?'

What happened?

She never accused me like the other foster parents. Somehow she saw the good in me when I could not see the good in myself.

At that point, I no longer got suspended from school. My grades began to improve, and I went from a D average to getting mostly B grades. Ms. Bell told me that God made me unique and that I had something to offer the world.

I began to believe her because she said it so much. Not only that, but I also watched how she treated others. She was kind and helped anyone in need. She didn't have to bully anyone into protecting them. It was not what she said, but it is how she acted. She was different from anyone I had ever known. People loved her! Living with Ms. Bell was the first time I experienced love. I did not change overnight. It was more of a gradual process with a lot of help from others.

Today, I want to give back that same help I received from others. I have two foster homes for girls. I only hire those who have a passion for lifting the girls, improving their self-esteem, and letting them know that they are unique. It will take time for some of the girls because the adults in their lives have let them down, and we must rebuild the trust. Because the girls have been moved from one pillar to one post, their trust meter is low and rightfully so.

I did not trust anyone until Ms. Bell. As a teenager, I decided to be a Ms. Bell in the lives of foster youth. Several young ladies who we fostered have graduated and have gone on to finish their college degrees. If you know anything about foster youth statistics, the U.S. Department of Health and Human Services Administration for Child Welfare says that fifty percent of foster youth will never graduate from high school or obtain a GED, and only fifteen percent of foster children will attend college. Fewer than three percent will earn a college degree.

We aim to see that each young lady has an opportunity for success, and maybe one day, they can pay it forward for the next.

Do you have any advice?

My advice is that you may not be handed the best life, but do the best with what you have. Somehow turn your pain into something useful that changes the lives of others!

Thank you for letting me share my story.

I thanked Marcy for her transparency and insight. Everyone is not given the same start in life. Each interview provides a glimpse into the power of words and actions and how they foster success or disappointment.

Life does not always come in a neat little package for some. It is the tenacity, the unquestionable grit, and determination that will see you through.

It does not matter how you start; it is how

you finish.

• • • • •

Chapter 3: Love Out Loud

1 Corinthians 13:4-5 states, *Love is patient, love is kind. It does not envy, it does not boast, it is not proud. It does not dishonor others, it is not self-seeking, it is not easily angered, it keeps no record of wrongs.*

There are many books written on love and relationships. One of the best known is *Men Are from Mars, Women Are from Venus* by John Gray, Ph.D. Dr. John Gray is a relationship counselor and a speaker who provides advice on navigating intimate relationships. Early in his book, Dr. Gray makes it clear that he is generalizing, explaining the differences between men and women, and how to navigate the differences and create ways to close the gaps.

Another book about love and relationships is *The Five Love Languages* by Dr. Gary Chapman, a marriage counselor who worked with hundreds of couples for over thirty-five years. Dr. Chapman reviewed twelve years of notes and noticed that the information fell into five categories: Words of Affirmation, Quality Time, Receiving Gifts, Acts of Service, and Physical Touch.

As a woman thinks, her mindset will dictate her future and life. What we focus on grows! If you think you can't, you are right—you won't. We become what we think about most of the time. Love is no different. If you believe you are worthy of a loving relationship, you will not run through stop signs or stop at the corner of Not The Right Street For You!

We embrace the love we believe we deserve.
— Pamela Hardy-Shepard

Leslie, 51 (*I met Leslie at the gym several years ago, and I asked her if she would be interested in being interviewed for this book. Before I could finish the sentence, Leslie said yes! I knew if anyone would share their thoughts on love, it would be Leslie.*)

I have been ready all my life for an opportunity to tell my story.

What does love mean to you?

Love means so many things, but to me, love means being in a loving relationship with a man having great communication, intimacy, romance, and being caught up in the present moment, a sense of humor, making time for one another, having a fluid household task and doing right by one another out of commitment.

I'm not sure what a fluid household means?

When I said fluid, I meant that either one of us could take on the household task. Like cooking, doing the dishes, laundry, and taking out the trash. We share the responsibility, and the household tasks are not assigned or expected because you are the woman or the man of the house.

How did you two arrive at a fluid household task?

Let me back up. I want you to know I do not get up on the roof to clean the gutters, but you better believe I am outside, holding the ladder and having some type of drink ready when my husband comes down the ladder.

I want my husband to know that I am there with him. When we are both at home, we work together and sometimes make a competition out of who will finish first. Usually, it's my husband, because I'm a little slow-moving, but it's so much fun to laugh about doing work. We make quality time with one another.

How do you do that?

We love each other. We take time for what is important, right?

Right!

We encourage one another in our relationship regarding the things we may want to do or problems with family or work. Sure, there are times I don't feel like doing the right thing, but I do it anyway! Love, to me, is a man who understands me and loves me despite my strengths and flaws.

I have heard of women mentioning their flaws, but you included strengths. Could you tell me more?

I am a strong woman. I know who I am and the talent and skills I possess. For some men, a beautiful, independent, intelligent, talented, and strong woman is a threat. That is why I included strength.

Why would you be a threat to your husband?

I will be very blunt right here: some women use their beauty as a bargaining chip. They know how to make their partner jealous. If you are beautiful, other men will look at you. One of the things I feel is, if you are in a relationship or married, make sure your man feels secure. Men can feel vulnerable in their relationship too! It is important to let him know that he is wanted by your words and actions! It is a must that women understand their man. Men are simple. They don't use coded messages like women. However, they have their own things that they do.

Love, to me, is a man I can trust and who will trust me right back. When I say trust, I mean the kind of trust you would die for. I know my husband has my best interests at heart and would never do anything to hurt me intentionally! He is my protector by day and my lover by night. He is my best friend. A best friend meaning we can share things together. This is not to say that he shares everything with me. There are some things he will not share; however, I can know just by observing.

When we talk, there is nothing off-limits in our relationship. We check our egos at the door. We are mature enough to hear and understand the truth without getting upset or mad. We keep an open mind to the other's perspective. We can talk for hours without cell phones or any type of social media to interrupt our conversation. If one of us is expecting a call or text, we say it up front. If a call comes in for either of us, we let it go to voicemail and get it later. Our life is right now! Not the job, my friends, his friends or even our family. We had to learn that 'we' are the priority.

With the change in technology, everyone wants your attention right now, and we had to change how we did things. When we got married, pagers were the thing. Later, cell phones played a big part. However, it cost more to use them, and the plans were crazy back then. Back then, we were charged morning, evening, or night plans. Now, children have cell phones. I feel all this technology is a distraction to relationships and families. I know my husband hears me, but he does not hear me all the time, and the same goes for me. We consistently strive to do better! It is a work in progress every day!

In our marriage, there are times we do not agree, and sometimes we are not agreeable, but we learned to work it out. There are times I say to myself, 'You are right!' But then I say to myself, 'Walk away, walk away,' and I ask myself two questions: Will this make a difference tomorrow or next week? Is it more important for me to be right or keep the peace? Sometimes my response to myself is, 'I don't care about next week or the peace! He thinks he knows everything!' But I come to myself most of the time. We both had to learn that love is give and take in a relationship. My husband has loved me through thick and thin, up and down, as I have loved him!

What keeps the love lights burning in your relationship?

Over the years, our bodies have changed. We both have more around our midsections than before. My husband tells me he loves all of me, including every stretch mark and dimple. He tells me I am perfect for him. It makes me feel special and like a million dollars! When we were first married, I would ask him about how I look in an outfit. He would glance up and say, 'You look fine.' He would say, 'Why do you continue to ask me? I said you look fine.'

(She stopped in the middle of her thought) I am so glad you are doing this book, because no woman wants to just look fine! We had to have a coming to Jesus meeting about when I ask, 'How do I look?' I want a real truthful answer, not something he thinks I want to hear! He said he was being truthful. I said, as your wife, I would like you to take in everything, hold it and then give your response. Notice my hair and outfit. Do I look beautiful, attractive, sexy to you? I want to know, so I can repeat the look! I explained when you say, 'Honey, you look fine,' I had to let him know that this is so hum-drum. But honey, when you say, 'You look hot!' it makes me take note of what you like and makes me walk on clouds!

When we were dating, my heart would race, and I would get that funny feeling in the pit of my stomach. Today, that funny feeling is replaced with the feeling of safety, always being connected, and knowing that he would not do anything to hurt me, and I him. I could not imagine it being any other way.

I want to share this with women. We teach our husbands, our children, our family, and our friends how to treat us. We all get a payoff for the way we behave. If the people in your life did not get something from it, they would do something differently. My husband and I had to teach each other how we would be treated. I would also like to say, how you acted with your last partner is in the past. Your man or woman is here in the present. Leave the past in the past; you may miss something in the present. That is why it is a gift!

I must tell you about my biggest pet peeve: electronic devices at dinner. Why go out to dinner if you or your mate will be surfing the web, looking at unimportant emails, Instagram, or Facebook? Stay home! I think electronic devices have their place. They are supposed to make our lives better, but do they really? Try no electronics Saturday or Sunday and see how it goes.

I thanked Leslie for her interview, which I found to be insightful and thought-provoking. Because of her insights, I talked to my own husband about a no device day. We started out with a half-day of no devices. Since that time, we have gone for seven days completely device-free! I must say, spending time together without distractions was incredibly romantic and special.

Considering Leslie's interview, it made me think about wanting a truthful opinion on how I look in a specific outfit. I have had the opportunity to discuss wanting a truthful opinion with several men, and most of the men indicated that some women do not want to know the truth. They don't want to cause hurt feelings or disagreements, so men will say what the woman wants to hear. However, some women can handle the truth and want nothing but the truth!

Can you handle the truth?

• • • • •

Candy, 46, single, budget analyst

What does love mean to you?

What does love mean to me? Thinking out loud, love is a feeling. It could be a noun or a verb. I will use it as a verb, a deep romantic and affectionate love that I feel for someone. I have never been married, so I don't know what it takes to stay in love for a long time. I figured it takes more than a feeling. As old as I am, I know it is not like the Cinderella story, happily ever after.

Why not?

I have girlfriends who are married, and some are happy and some are not. Some stay in their marriages because of the way they are used to living. Others are happy because they figured out how to be happy. Not being married, I can only speculate. Love is a commitment; it is being with someone that you are evenly yoked with.

What does evenly yoked mean?

It means that you both must be on the same page, such as your values, spirituality, your faith, finances, gratitude, being positive, raising a family, etc. I would not think seriously about a man that does not love his mother, and I would not be with a man who allows his mother to interfere in our relationship. So, I say, love means many things. In the meantime, I will continue to love myself by making me happy.

Could you tell me a little more about making yourself happy?

An immediate example that comes to mind is taking a class on bartending, cooking, glass blowing, or Zen gardening. I like trying new things, and it brings me such joy!

What does happiness mean to you?

Happiness, to me, is doing all the things that are important for me, liking the way I look and feel. In my job, I must feel valued to be happy. I'm happy when I spend time with my friends, just to talk. I'm happy having the opportunity to go out with the girls for weekend shopping, getting our nails done, or having lunch. I love to get facials and massages. Basically, I will date myself. If I cannot do it for myself, why should a man do it for me?

Oh, one other thing—it is about giving back to others, so I volunteer several places in the community!

One day, the right person for me will appear. In the meantime, I will continue to work on me! My spirituality, my health, and my profession. I'm not looking for anyone. When you look, you never find. I will get me in order, so when he shows up, I will be ready.

I was amazed by and grateful for Candy's awareness. It has been my experience that many women expect their partners to make them happy. When couples are dating, they put their best foot forward. The person attracted to you appreciated your value, your appearance, and your independence. You both were enjoying life in your particular way. No one wants to be with a handsome man or a beautiful woman who complains all the time, or someone who only brings negative energy. My mother would always say, 'Pretty is as pretty does.' Meaning your actions are more important than your looks.

Love reveals the concealment of who we really are,

exposing that beauty is only skin deep.

— Pamela Hardy-Shepard

• • • • •

Karen, 50, married, administrative assistant

What does love mean to you?

What love means to me? It means that I am respected and valued by my husband, family, and friends. I included family and friends because I love them as well, just different from my husband. Early in our marriage, my husband and I learned that we communicate very differently. It was an area of contention for a while. We had to work on it as if our lives depended upon it. We started out by discussing our common interests and goals. We made a specific time to discuss finances, home issues, and family needs. We don't discuss those things when either of us had just come in the door from work. The time we spent communicating, the less time we complained! Because of better communication and learning to focus on what really matters, we fell deeper in love. We began doing activities such as kayaking and going to theatrical performances and comedy shows. We would even play board games and shut the rest of the world out. We laugh a lot, sometimes over nothing. To keep our love strong, we provide each other what the other needs.

I am interested in learning what made you both shift?

Great question. One night, we got into a two-and-a-half-hour argument over free time and how we spend it. I wanted to do something other than sit around the house and watch TV. From our last argument, we both realized we had to do something different then what we have been doing, or we might be heading for divorce court. We confirm what we hear from each other to ensure we heard the other correctly.

You are really making me think. I have always thought my husband was handsome. He just gets more handsome to me the longer we are married. I really think it is the way I think about him. Most days, I take time to compliment my husband before he leaves for work. I write him little sexy notes that only he and I understand.

This is what I have to say to the women who will read this book. This is where most of us do not get it. Your husband goes out into the world every day. He is surrounded by women all day who may find him attractive or kind. For the most part, his coworkers are women, and some may be attractive. If these women are not in a great relationship, they may want what you have. Make sure you are the one complimenting him. Make sure you are the one that tells him he looks and smells good. You are the one that tells him how smart he is or how you appreciate him before he leaves or when he gets home. If he beats you home each day, pat your powder and add your lipstick. I'm sure once some women read this part, they are probably saying, 'Why? I'm going home.' I would say to those women, you make sure you brush your teeth at lunch, right? If you wear makeup, you reapply your makeup during the day for people you don't love. Surely you can do it for your husband. If you are home each day, make sure you don't look how you looked when he left in the morning. Take a shower or bath before he arrives, put on some makeup, fix your hair and put on some perfume. Smell good for your man.

Stop complaining about what he has done for you lately! I want to ask your readers: 'What have you done for him lately?' Everything is not about you! One last thing, if you think you are going to change him—good luck with that! When you are complaining, he is listening and taking mental notes. Women have so much influence over our husbands and families. Use your influence in a positive way that makes him a better man. Men change because their hearts tell them to do so, not your nagging and complaining about what he does not do right. I'm not saying that your complaints are not justified. But focus on what he does right, and guess what, ladies? He will do more of it! You have the power to change your household! Your words and actions matter! He knows who you are: the good, the bad, and the ugly!

Karen's interview calls for each of us to look in the mirror at ourselves. Her words are a call to action to examine our beliefs, thought, and actions. My favorite part of the interview was when she spoke the truth and said, 'If you think you will change him, good luck with that.'

> *We cannot change anyone but ourselves; when you change you, everyone else will change. Become the change you wish to see!*

● ● ● ● ●

Lydia, 45, single, fundraiser

Tell me what love means to you?

This may sound negative, but it means you are going to get screwed physically and figuratively!

(I was ready for Lydia's brutal honesty, and I asked her to provide some additional insight.)

I have been in numerous relationships where men smile to your face and do all of the little things you want them to do, and all along, their intent is to get you in the bed and have their way. This is not to say that there are not good men. I'm telling you what my experience has been. When I meet a man I think I'm interested in, I have learned not to talk about my past or how someone treated me. What I have learned about some men is that they begin by saying sweet nothings or communicating the way they think

I would like when it is not their style. Today, communication is organic. I really want to know who they are as individuals. I listen more than ever before. I listen to how they communicate with friends or about how their relationship ended. I want an authentic relationship. I will not jump in bed without knowing a person first. This means the person I am dating will not be coming to my house for six months, and I will not be going to his house.

Why six months?

This allows me to get to see who they really are, and they can do the same. What I have learned is that he is going to treat me the way I treat myself. I am worthy of love, real love. But first, I must love myself. If a man is not willing to stay around and date me under those circumstances, then he is not the one for me. I want to see him through all seasons. Earlier, I sounded so negative, but I wanted whoever is reading this book to know that they do not have to lose who they are to be in a relationship. Women, we are the crown glory of any man; first, we must know it!

Is there anything else you would like to share?

Yes, stop being arm candy for men who don't honor or love you! Ladies, use your brains. Why would a man be interested in marrying you if you have given him the entire store! All any man can do for me is visit the store and see what the store has to offer. No one comes to the store and tries out the products on the shelves and then leaves the store without paying. A purchase is necessary.

I was blown away by Lydia's analogy of love and relationships. I thanked her for her perception and honesty.

Relationships are good for the soul; they force us to open our hearts, knowing that there is a possibility that our hearts may be broken one day. When the heart is open, we have the opportunity to experience life on another level, another plane. Love relationships provide a warmth that cannot be found alone. — Pamela Hardy-Shepard

• • • • •

Chapter 4: Sex and Power

Look at you; you are as sexy as you please.

When you walk in a room, all the men freeze.

They can only see you with their eyes.

Because you have mastered the great compromise.

— Pamela Hardy-Shepard

Relaxing in my cozy, comfortable slippers, feeling a sense of security, I began to reread the Sexy as You Please poem, thinking about my own sexiness. I can honestly say, there was not a time when I walked in a room and all of the men paused. As women, we are seen for our beauty first and then our brains. *Did I ever feel sexy?* I think I felt sexy at different times in my life. *What about you?*

• • • • •

Amanda, 50, single, teacher

Who taught you about sex and pleasure?

To answer your first question, no one taught me about my period. I learned about where babies came from, and that is it! I think my mother was afraid to really tell me about sexual pleasure because of how she was raised in the church, or she really did not know herself. Honestly, I think my mother did not know how to talk to me or simply really did not know anything other than what her mother taught her. I bet if you were to ask one hundred women who taught them about sex, they will say their mothers. But really, they did not teach them about sex; they taught them the function of the body. I did not see my parents get intimate, and when I say intimate, I mean a long embrace or a passionate kiss. They showed me that they love me by kissing and hugging me, but their behavior did not reflect that of each other. Their behavior was always appropriate. 'Hi, honey,' a peck on the lips or cheek. I think I would have viewed things differently if my father came in the door from work and embraced my mother before he sat down to unwind.

I want to be sure I'm hearing you correctly. You feel that your parents' behavior was always appropriate around you. Like your father pecking your mother on the lips or cheek. You would have preferred to see something different every now and then?

Yes, one that I could see and do myself.

Do you think not seeing your parents have an outward expression of love impacts you?

Yes, I do.

In what way?

It would have been good to know what a loving relationship looked like. I peck my husband in the same way my parents kissed each other in front of us. I don't think they should have been drooling all over each other every day in front of us, but some real passion would not have hurt us from time to time! I was told a long time ago we tend to replicate some of our parents' behavior. Just look around; you can find this anywhere!

How do I feel about sex? I love sex! I love how it makes me feel as a woman. I feel special and close to my partner. Most importantly, I need to say, I love me and what I have to offer in a relationship. I think it is a way to connect and be one with that person. Hopefully, the person you connect with on that level is worthy of your gold between your legs!

What advice would you give to younger women about sexual relationships?

I think women go into intimate sexual relationships thinking it is going to be the most wonderful experience. I hate to burst your bubble, but for many women, it is not. I would tell younger women to explore their bodies first before having sex. A woman needs to know what she likes. Know how to pleasure yourself first! Know the areas that please you. In our society, we don't discuss women pleasuring themselves. What we do see portrayed on TV and in books is young boys experimenting and learning about their bodies. Their behavior is seen as normal, natural, and common. However, in stark contrast, it is not the same for young girls. There is nothing about them being in control of their bodies. What we see in this society is that men, including their sexuality, control women. Watch any show on TV, and you will see this played out in every case.

Some women expect that a man is going to know what their needs are. It would be best if you told men what you need. If he is an observant man, he will know what your needs are. Many women fall into casual sex with men because they look for love in all of the wrong places. Women, you love yourself, date yourself, please yourself! You don't want to be with every Tom, Dick, or Harry! If you are going to have sex, take your time, and pick your partner carefully. Every time you have sex with someone, you are having sex with everyone they have slept with as well.

I know this may be hard for some women, but I'm telling you to really look at his penis. Make sure that it has no bumps or smells funny. I was told by my uncle to put alcohol on my hands and rub his penis, avoiding the opening, to make sure there are no open sores on the shaft or the surrounding area. And for your sake, make sure he wraps it up. Take no chances. The same goes for you. Whoever you have sex with leaves a little bit of himself with you. If he will not wrap it up, insist on it or no sex. The decision you make today may be with you for the rest of your life! I'm sharing with you because I had to learn the hard way! There were no books at that time telling me I had the power over my sexual self!

Enough of that. But the truth is, one day, you will no longer be young, footloose and fancy-free. Everything changes! Starting with your hormones, possibly your sex drive too! Fortunately, you can start thinking about how to prevent this early. One way is to treat your body like a temple. The way God made it to be! By the time you get my age and older, sex is like an oven that needs to be turned on to bake a cake. For me, sex begins each morning, by the words and actions from my partner. It takes some of us a longer time to get started. Once we get the oven turned on and heated up, the cake can begin to bake. Something to think about—if these things are happening to you, maybe they are happening to your partner. As men age, they lose testosterone and go through a man-o-pause or midlife crisis.

(Amanda sounded agitated as she continued.)

My doctor told me that my hormones will slow down; estrogen and progesterone levels will fluctuate. He said some women may experience decreased libido. I was shocked, and asked, 'What can I do?' My doctor told me that he could prescribe Hormone Replacement Therapy.

I asked my doctor, 'Could you please tell me about this, and what will the side effect be?' My doctor looked at me and said just because my mother had breast cancer, there is no evidence I will get cancer by using Hormone

Replacement Therapy. He also told me that he can prescribe me an anti-depressant. I immediately felt offended, and I said, 'I have hot flashes. I am not depressed! Thank you, but no thank you!' Unfortunately, my doctor did not tell me about the research or state the reason for prescribing antidepressants.

Listen, ladies, this is your body. Do not leave it to your doctor only. You are the advocate for your sexual health and your mental health—period! After doing a little research and talking to some of my most trusted friends, I found supplements that help me with hot flashes, dryness, and my desire to have sex. I enjoy sex more now than when I was younger.

Why is that?

I don't have to worry about becoming pregnant. And being more mature, I am more authentic with myself and my partner. When I was younger, it was the pressure of … just do it! Today, there is no pressure or the stress of being perfect. If I'm not interested in the moment, I do not—will not—succumb to any advances. What is most important to me is being emotionally connected and being close to my partner. I will initiate sex and feel confident in doing so. If he says, 'I have a headache,' I smile and remember those days.

This is something I want other women to think about. As men get older, especially older than me, some men might have erectile dysfunction problems. For most men, it is too embarrassing to discuss it. I am not a man; however, a lot of their ego, pride, and joy is being able to perform sexually—something we women have no concept. I'm happy that some of the stigma is being lifted for men through commercials and education.

I also enjoy being with younger men for their hard bodies and sexual attitudes; however, there is a tradeoff. Some of the younger men think they know everything about how a woman's body works, and I find myself doing a lot of teaching, showing younger men to slow down and be tender and thoughtful with their partner. I feel sex is an important connection but not the only connection. When you write your next book, I can let you know how my committed relationship has panned out. I think he is the one.

One last thing I want to say: I have often thought having sex with different partners does more harm than good. Let me explain. I often question if I'm being compared to a previous lover, or will I compare my committed relationship to a previous relationship. Well, I will not know until we become committed.

Are you comparing now?

I don't mean to do it, but I do.

What will be different when you get married?

(Amanda got quiet. I could tell she was thinking.)

I will have to get back to you on that!

Amanda's interview reminded me of how our society has changed. Fifty years ago, Amanda's interview would have been X-rated, and my writing it in a book would have been unacceptable.

In the 1970s, a traditional family was a married couple with children and grandparents who lived close by. One of the results of this family dynamic was that the older women would prepare the younger women for life. Preparing the younger women for life meant the M-word: Marriage! The main topics of the big M word included raising a family, housework, and cooking. Depending on the women (mother or grandmother), their thoughts and discussions might have even been discrete discussions on how to behave as a woman in a relationship with intimacy and sex.

The survey I conducted revealed that depending on when you were born, mothers did not discuss how to take care of their womanly parts with their Baby Boomer daughters. They also did not talk about the art of sensual pleasure and owning your desire to have sex. A very surprising part of the survey revealed Generation X had more information than their Baby Boomer counterparts. However, the survey also showed that cultural differences played a significant role in sexual attitudes handed down through generations. The survey also indicated that Generation X was more willing to discuss sex, regardless of social and cultural differences, than the Baby Boomer generation.

Because of fundamental changes in family dynamics, the Women's Liberation Movement, and the migration of women into the workplace, the typical family has been reshaped. Families have moved across the country, divorce rates have increased, and personal lifestyle choices have led to lives where grandparents are no longer prevalent in mainstream society. Because of the changing dynamic, women have had to get support from the internet, magazines, blogs, TV shows, podcasts, and each other. The advice from magazines and TV is not always the best resource, as you will see in my interview with Rebecca.

• • • • •

Rebecca, 48, in her second marriage of two years

(Rebecca is a very private woman, but she was willing to share her story to help others.)

You asked about having power in the bedroom or the world. When I was younger, and in my first marriage, having power was not the case for me. I did not have power in the world or in the bedroom, at least none that I was aware of at the time.

The life I was living was less than powerful. What possible power could I yield? I was young and naïve; my ex-husband demanded things to be his way. When we were dating, I overlooked many red flags. I was married to a selfish and controlling man. He controlled everything in our lives: what we ate, when we ate, where I could go, and what friends we had. He even controlled our sex. He determined what day and which position. Reflecting, sex was strictly for his pleasure, and my enjoyment was none of his concern or my business. I didn't even know I was supposed to have an orgasm. In my mind, I wondered what an orgasm would feel like. I was too embarrassed to ask anyone or even attempt to pleasure myself, because I was raised to believe that was a taboo. There was no power or pleasure for me in our bedroom. Sex was not what I thought it would be, and it took a divorce and many years later to learn what I was missing.

Once I learned and experienced the pleasure of shared commitment of love and joy, I could not get enough sexual pleasure from my partner. If I had any advice for younger women, first, pick the right partner—one that will show sensitivity to your needs. When you are dating, pay attention to the small things. Do not overlook specific behavior and make excuses. 'Oh, he is under a lot of stress at work, he is not always like that.' Listen to your most trusted family and friends. Are there objections? What kind of objections? Step back and see if the objections from others might be true. Pray and ask God to show you if this is the man you want to spend the rest of your life with. Is he kind in front of others and then is gruff in private, or uses words that hurt? All these things will show up in your married life as well!

How do you know your future husband will be a great sexual partner?

Physically, you will not know, but one way is his communication. Pay attention to how a man communicates. Does he get frustrated when you don't understand his communication or when you ask questions? Does he always have to be right? I want you to think about what I just said, ladies.

You see, for women, good sex starts when you get up in the morning, by the words and the way you communicate with one another. If you cannot communicate about the day-to-day things, how will you communicate how you want to be touched? Will he be as sensitive to your needs as you are to his needs?

You must experience pleasure in sex. As a mature woman, it is my responsibility to share my story about my lack of sexual knowledge with other women, hoping not one more woman must fake enjoying sex or say in their head, 'Is he done yet?' If things had been different, I would not have had to spend several years feeling numb and misinformed about sex. Today, I don't know if mothers are teaching or informing their daughters about giving pleasure and receiving pleasure. Well, if mothers are not providing this information, where are younger women getting their information? Movies, magazines, porn? It is not real! I think some of the problems in sexual relationships are that many men are looking at porn and trying to put this in their day-to-day lives. You don't want a man that tries to play out his porn fantasies on you.

It would have been best for me to have learned from my mother, to be told how to enjoy my future husband's touch and to be able to give that touch as well. A mother can only teach her daughter what she knows. There is a saying: 'It takes a village to raise a child.' Well, in this case, no one from my village told me as a young girl how to ask for what I needed.

Rebecca's words rang loud and clear in my ears. With that said, this book is the village; the stories allow women to support one another by telling their truth. Women have many advantages over men because of our nurturing nature and socialization. We have BFFs, sisters, and girlfriends to give emotional support when we need it. We just have to know who to ask, and treasure them when we find them.

• • • • •

Lacy, 63, married, Chef

Lacy is a confident woman who knows what she wants out of life. The interview began with Lacy telling me she is free, expressive, and happy to share.

I know who I am as a woman, and I certainly know my worth. I enjoy life to the fullest. My life has not always been this way. I had to work on myself to obtain this confidence level. When I was a younger woman, I was in a relationship with a man who was from a different culture and country. He was handsome and very charming early on in our relationship, but he attempted to dominate me and our relationship as time went on. I stayed in that relationship for eleven months. During that time, I watched and listened. Many of my friends warned me, but I figured they did not know what they were talking about—until I saw how he treated his sister. I realized then that the women in his culture took a back seat, and the men ruled everything. In my heart of hearts, I knew this relationship was not for me. At first, it wasn't easy to let the relationship go, because I liked him a lot and we had chemistry. He was a great lover, and he was the jam on my toast.

(She laughed and then sighed as though her mind went there for a moment.)

I am married, and I have a man on the side. I love my husband very much! He loves me, as well. I know this sounds cliché, but sometimes love is not enough. Sex is something that my husband cannot give me due to an accident, so I seek sex elsewhere. My man on the side is single and wants no entanglements, so our relationship works well for both of us. Both of our sexual needs are met, and I want for nothing. I don't want anyone to judge me until you walk in my shoes.

My husband does not have a clue about my extramarital affair, and he would die if he did. I do everything in my power to make sure he does not have any idea. I would never forgive myself if he found out.

My husband can be tender, but I think he gets frustrated because we cannot have intercourse. He does his best to give me pleasure, but he gets nothing from the encounter, in my opinion. I cannot imagine how he must feel as a man. I often think back to when my husband could perform sexually and how our life was then. The man he was then and the man he has become is quite different. I do not think he has come to terms with how our life is now. At times, I have not either. In the quiet of the night, I pray and hope God will forgive me of my sins.

It seems as though you have a lot going on in your life. How do you keep it all together?

I categorize each part of my life. At first, it was not easy to do, but I learned to create a routine that is easy to follow. I still work, which is a plus because it gives me a reason to leave the house each day. Once I have a routine, I do not deviate. I fix dinner every night, or my husband will help me. At times, my job may require me to travel, and at those times, I get together with my man on the side.

Who taught you about sex and pleasure? How do you feel about sex as a woman? What advice would you provide to a younger woman about sexual relationships? What do women need to know about their sexuality?

Wow, who taught me about sex and pleasure? Well, when I was younger, I would say to myself, there has got to be more to sex than this! When I was eighteen, sex was disappointing. The guy I was sleeping with would come as soon as he put his penis in. He was terrible, and I would lay there, wondering if it would ever get better. It was a process over the years. Men taught me about sex and pleasure. I did not learn it from my mother or a book. Men taught me what was pleasing over the years. The sad part is that I did not know myself.

I don't want the entire interview to focus on my sexual life, though, because my life is full. I love to read and do crossword puzzles. I love music and share my love with my husband. My husband and I love to cook gourmet meals and invite our friends over and enjoy an evening of good food, good wine, and great company.

To answer your question about what advice I can provide to a younger woman about a sexual relationship, I would say to younger women: You must first enjoy your life now, because tomorrow your life could change forever. Learn from all your mistakes. Always be thinking about being a better person. Sexually, know that this is your body, and you are responsible for your pleasure.

I thanked Lacy for her openness and letting us women know that we can enjoy sex for years to come. As women, it is okay to enjoy sex as long as you want or can.

• • • • •

Chapter 5: Life's Influence

One of the roles of influence is to 'be the voice' for the voiceless. — Pamela Hardy-Shepard

• • • • •

Marlene, 46, single, attorney

Who influenced you to become an attorney?

This is easy! As a young teen, I worked summers for three years for an attorney. At first, I just filed papers. The next summer, I filed papers and answered the phones. The third year, I could drive, so I would run errands to the courthouse. I felt what I was doing was important, just like the attorney. All I could see at the time was how the attorney that I worked for helped people change their lives for the best. After high school, I went to college and earned my bachelor's degree in sociology. I studied and passed the Law School Admission Test. I attended law school and earned my Juris Doctor. I began clerking at a local law firm and studied for my state bar examination, and here I am. If I had not spent those three summers working for an attorney, I don't think I would be a family attorney now. As a teenager, I did not know the influence my boss, the paralegals, and clients would have on me. I've done my best to pay it forward by holding shadowing for high school students twice a year. I also have job shadowing for law students as well!

What would you tell young women?

I tell young women this: You have a purpose on this earth! You can be what you want. Do not let anyone tell you what you can or cannot be in this world. Remember, this is your life's work. It is important to look around and learn what possibilities are out there for you.

There is a book that I recommend for all the female students who shadow me. This book could also help women who want to make a change in their lives: *The Girl's Guide to the Big Bold Moves for Career Success*. The book provides a roadmap to help women find their way in their work lives. As women, we must help one another in our lives! As women, we look to our mothers and others who charge ahead or who have laid the groundwork for change. Historically, there have been women influencers who have inspired us. When you were born determines who influenced you as a woman.

For me, Debbie Allen and the TV show *Fame* were the most important influences in my life. Debbie Allen was a powerful and very multi-talented woman; we all wanted to be just like her. She demanded excellence from her students, and they produced each week. Her drive and ambitions spoke to my heart that you could be and do what you love with excellence! I was also influenced by the Cosby family, watching a successful doctor and lawyer raising a family and community members. Their lives were filled with love and devotion to each other and their family. Even when they disagreed, they were agreeable. They were funny and fun to watch, but most importantly, they were smart! Those two shows had an impact on me as a young girl. I learned from each of the shows I mentioned that I can love what I do.

In life, we will never know who is watching us. It could be your spouse, your child, colleagues, or your neighbor down the street. Every day I smile at strangers, and most of the time, strangers smile back at me. We emit our emotions and inner thoughts via our words and actions, even from the quietest and smallest. Nothing can encourage us like someone else's good example. They are frankly few and far between—but they are essential.

Do you want to create value with your life? Become a good influence. It was Gandhi who said be the change you wish to see. In a world of divisiveness, a morning smile or wave goes a long way. I decided early on in my life I would be the change; it starts with me. I cannot wait for others to change the world. Women have so much power in our world. It is sad when I hear women discuss their jobs, relationships, and family issues like they cannot fix them or have limited power over them. Historically, women have always been a collective reckoning force. Women have always raised each other with compassionate support to make changes in the world!

Marlene's interview outlined so many things that women do daily without thought. We women collaborate, negotiate, communicate effectively, solve problems and critically analyze situations. We lead by example, we are visionaries, and we provide positive reinforcement to those around us. We love hard and we love softly. We encourage, have a God-given intuition, have faith, and are spiritually strong.

I have my cape—what about you?

• • • • •

Sophia, 49, recently divorced, seventeen-year-old son

(I did not need to ask Sofia any questions. She was ready to provide her advice as soon as we started talking!)

Women, life is short, and it is time to get your act together! By now, each of you has experienced life's ups and downs in some way, so here is my advice. Live your life like there is no tomorrow! Check your mindset. Is it a growth or fixed mindset? A growth mindset is one that believes all things are possible, accepts and embraces challenges and sees them as a way that makes you stronger; these women persist in the face of obstacles. Women with a growth mindset believe that obstacles are a way to learn and grow from the experience. These women search for the silver lining in every problem. In contrast, women with a fixed mindset hold a pessimistic view of things. The glass is half empty instead of half full concept. Why is this happening to me? If not you, then who? It is not what happens to us in life, but our reaction to what happens to us! Get up, dust yourself off, and try once more! It could be your job, your home, a relationship, your children, your weight, or a hobby. Whatever it is, do not quit! Do not give in!

Many people say what they want to do, but they are unwilling to do what it takes to get their dream. It may appear to happen overnight, and for others, it may seem to take some time. I love movies, and there is a movie that is an example of how things are not always perfect, but in the end, the dream is realized: *The Count of Monte Christo* by Alexandre Dumas. In the movie, Edmond Dantes, a merchant sailor, has a dream to be a ship's Captain, marry his fiancé, and live a happy life. Then, his dreams are stolen by his jealous friend who has riches, stature, and every material blessing. The story ends with a reversal of fortune, when Edmond, after more than twelve years, gets back the love of his life, status, and riches. The story shows love and hope.

Sofia's interview is an example of the resiliency of women. The Count of Monte Christo provides a backdrop of the importance of finding the silver lining in one's life. Sofia is correct. What you focus on grows. It is incredible how powerful our beliefs and thoughts can be, and how our circumstances can determine our happiness and lives. Henry Ford once said, 'Whether you think you can, or you think you can't—you're right.'

As the commencement speaker at the University of Maryland, Deshauna Barber passionately told her story of how she lost six Miss USA competitions and managed to come back for the seventh time and become the first soldier to gain the title of Miss USA in 2016. Each example depicts the importance of never quitting. Commit to what you say you want. Only you can stop you!

Your NO is a YES deferred!

• • • • •

Chapter 6: Yesterday, Today, and Tomorrow

As a young girl in the second grade, I would hear my mother say, 'Watch, listen, and observe; you may learn something.' I listened to my mother's advice. I would go to school and watch my classmates during recess. Despite our assumptions that mean girl behavior is strictly a pubescent high school trait, I witnessed girls being cruel to their classmates as early as second grade. There was a little clique of mean girls in my school who would not let girls who looked different play with them, and I was one of those girls who was not able to play. That's when I officially started observing my second-grade classmates having conversations on the playground from afar. I could see the girls discussing their twirling techniques and who could twirl the best on the bars.

As I matured, I began observing everyone! I would watch and listen to conversations between people in the grocery store, at church, and in the workplace. Because of the information I gleaned from observing, I thought it would be great to teach my children and my students this skill.

As a professor, I would ask my students probing questions to help them think critically and question everything. Once I gave my students in human services an assignment to go into a place of business, like a restaurant, bookstore or coffee shop, and unobtrusively observe two people having a conversation. I told them to watch the two individuals' body language, facial expressions, tone of voice, and speech patterns, and decide what type of conversation the two individuals might be having based on their assessment.

At first, the students thought this would be another tedious, meaningless assignment. It turned out to be one of their favorites! In class the next night, students fought over who would go first to tell what they learned. This assignment helped students sharpen their observation skills for personal life and the future clients they will be serving. Every student in the class discovered the importance of observation and how sharpening this skill would assist them throughout the rest of their lives.

As one student put it, 'I see the world differently now.'

Throughout the interviews for this book, I observed several common themes emerge: technological advances, such as poor face-to-face communication; parental lack of communication; and the decline of social skills. Because of the emerging themes, I wanted to know: How have the advances in technology changed the way we share information with other women?

• • • • •

Nancy, 56, married, chiropractor

Nancy, could you please share with me how you think technology changed how we share information with younger women?

This is an interesting question! I believe that things drastically changed when everyone started getting their cell phones. At first, it was a status symbol having a cell phone. I don't know how anyone could afford a cell phone back then; the plans were ridiculous. Most people probably don't even remember trying to save their minutes or wait until nighttime to call family and friends. In the early 2000s, the attitude changed regarding phones, the economy of scale happened, and everyone had a cell phone. I believe the change took place with texting and social media. The change wasn't even noticeable. We traded our phone calls for text messages and communicating on social media.

Technology changed spending time with friends as well. When we hang out, some may say, 'I need to check my messages,' meaning their text and social media post. Others say nothing and spend their time together surfing Instagram and Facebook.

Nowadays, individuals are not taking pictures to simply create memories; they are taking pictures to put on Facebook and Instagram. When we go out to dinner, I casually look around the room, and people of all ages have their phones in front of their faces. It's sad. Nothing is as important as the person in front of you! Yet we spend more time on computers, tablets, cell phones, and social media than we do with the people we say we love!

With everyone you encounter in life, you have a relationship—whether it is the man at a 7-Eleven or the teller at a bank. For each person that you encounter, whether it's for a brief second or years, value each encounter and know for sure whatever you send out is returned to you. Your messages can wait five minutes. Checking your Facebook can wait five minutes. Your life is right now! The urgency to post the picture or statement, will it matter five months from now? Whose life will it change? Your time is valuable; it is the one thing you will never get back. You must wisely choose how your time will be used—meaning relationships, friendships, and hanging out. Another thing, don't let anyone or things tie up your time. In other words, pick and choose your relationships, friends, and projects carefully.

• • • • •

Becky Ann, 58, married, dental assistant

How has technology changed the way you navigate your life?

Wow! I have a love/hate relationship with technology. The changes in technology have made our lives easier and more complicated at the same time. I remember using a pager! I thought this was the coolest thing! I started with a regular pager then upgraded to a Motorola pager that could leave messages other than a phone number. I can remember putting my pager on vibrate while in class in my backpack, and the pager would vibrate and scare me. During my college classes, if your pager went off in class, the professor would ask you to leave. Those days seemed like yesterday. So much has changed since those times.

(I could hear a tone of reflection in Becky Ann's voice.) How do you feel about the change?

When we are at a specific time in our lives, I think we don't appreciate where we are until we look back. To me, those were the best days of my life. Things seemed to be simpler back then. Today, things have to happen right away! Responses are needed from your boss, husband, and friends. I love and hate text messages. I love them because I can communicate my thoughts right away, but I hate them because they demand a response from me or the person receiving the message. We all know that everyone, for the most part, has a cell phone. When someone leaves a text message, you see it. People know when you read it, and you cannot say, 'Oh, I didn't see it.' To me, this is an added stressor. For young people, you have nothing else to compare your life to without technology.

We discussed changes you made in your life. Could you share a little?

I did some introspection and counseling to change the way I view life. When I changed on the inside of me, the outside changed as well. I used to be a very jealous, envious type of person. No one wanted to be around me; I did not want to be around myself. I was not happy unless there was some type of drama going on. I lost many friends because of my jealousy, thinking someone was flirting with my boyfriend or getting upset that my friend bought a new car and didn't tell me first. I knew I needed help when it spilled over into my job. It took many years to realize I had to change, no one else. Getting help relieved me of all kinds of stressors. I no longer felt that I had to compete or be the center of attention. I learned that the world did not revolve around me.

Thank you for sharing this very intimate detail. What advice would you provide any woman?

If you are unhappy, depressed, or if you are having problems at home or work—you are not alone. Seek help, reach out to a friend or family. Our mental health is as important as our physical health. You have only one life, live it well. Oh, and don't let technology invade your entire life! Do things that don't require technology. It may change your life.

Becky Ann's interview sheds light on the importance of emotional health. You do not have to live with emotional pain. Help is just a phone call away. Technology has made counseling available from the comfort of your home.

• • • • •

Cassie, 67, married photographer

How has technology changed your life?

It has changed my life a lot! I can remember as far back as when our house had a party line. For those young people who don't know what a party line is, we had to share a phone line with strangers. If you picked up the phone in your house, someone else might be talking on the line. It was a line-share service by multiple users that you did not know.

Back then, this is how telephone service was provided. We thought nothing of it because this was the way it was. Thinking back, people talked more to each other. People made visits to your home. We spent more time together as a family, extended family, and friends.

Today, I don't have to call you and get into a long, drawn-out conversation; I can send a text and tell you what I have to say. The best thing is that I no longer must use a Thomas Brothers map to find directions to my destination. I can either select the directions on my cell phone using WAZE, Google, or the maps apps or use the navigation system. I can also hit a button and call OnStar to guide me where I need to go. Yes, things have changed for the better in most cases, and some things have changed for the worse.

Could you tell me more about the things that have changed for the worse?

First, let me start with the children. Our children are addicted to cell phones, tablets, and games!

As a child, I can remember when it was not a good thing to sit too close to the TV. We were continuously told to scoot back away from the TV. Today, babies, children, and teens have their devices right up in their faces.

Parents don't seem to mind if it keeps the kids happy and out of their hair. I have been in the grocery store and seen babies who can barely sit in the grocery cart, but they have some little device playing so mom can shop. Hmmm, I took my children to the store, and they were merely okay. I did not appease them with buying special treats or some little trinket.

In time the truth will come out about the dangers of cell phones on children's little brains and bodies. My concern is that these kids are not finished growing, and their spines aren't either. I would like to see these same children's posture when they reach my age.

Now let me tell you about the young and older adults. Both groups have lost their minds. Whenever the phone makes a whiz, ding, or ring, they have to pick it up and see who sent them a text, email, or some notification from a platform. I wish I had a penny for every time I watched family members, friends, and people I don't even know walk around with their phones in their hands like the phone were gold. I guess it is gold, because we put our entire life on the phone. Remember the American Express commercial, Don't Leave Home Without It? Well, the algorithm that these developers created makes sure YOU don't.

Cassie's interview caused me to pause and think about how technology has changed my life. I can work on my computer and vacuum my entire upstairs without moving a muscle. Technology has made my life easier in many ways, and somewhat lazy and dependent on it.

Do you remember when you memorized everyone's phone number? Do you remember when you knew every street name within a four- to five-block radius? As much as I love technology for all the things it allows me to do, I still revert to writing all of my phone numbers down in an address book.

In what ways has technology changed your life?

• • • • •

Chapter 7: What is Your Legacy?

As you live each day, leave your mark on the
world through word or deed.
— Pamela Hardy-Shepard

According to the Merriam-Webster Dictionary, a legacy is a gift by will, especially of money or other personal property, or something transmitted by or received from an ancestor or predecessor or from the past.

When I interviewed women about the legacy they intend to leave behind, I found this question to be as daunting as the question about sex. At first, I was not getting anywhere with this question. Therefore, to start the conversation, I decided to ask each woman who their female hero was growing up. Some heroes were real people like Frida Kahlo, Sojourner Truth, Eleanor Roosevelt, and Rosa Parks; other heroes were Wonder Woman and Cat Woman. After asking that question, I then asked, 'What do you and your hero have in common?' Interestingly enough, the most repeated answer was that their hero was smart, knew how to get things done, and was brave and creative.

• • • • •

Nicole, 55, single, graphic designer

What legacy will you leave for your family?

I love that question; no one has ever asked me that question before. Plus, I never really gave much thought to what legacy I'm leaving behind. I'm no Anne Frank or Florence Nightingale. I'm just a normal person, doing normal things in life.

You don't think those women were normal people?

Hell no, I think they were special people.

What makes a special person?

I don't know; they have a gift or something.

You have a gift! You are an artist and a graphic artist, right?

Yes, I guess I'm special too.

(She laughed, and then was suddenly quiet for about thirty seconds. It seemed to last forever.)

When I think about a legacy, I would have to say my artwork.

That's a great example. Is there anything else?

I know I've been an example to my family and friends when I show them a good time. Is that a legacy?

It is. When we spend quality time with our loved ones, we leave a legacy of the heart.

I do one other thing—I feed the hungry. Because I talked so much about feeding hungry families, I was able to convince my family and some of my friends to donate too! Wow! I do have a legacy!

At that moment, I could tell Nicole was amazed at her outpouring of love, time, and money to support others. What are the things that you do each day and give no thought?

What bright light are you shining in the darkness to help others find their purpose?

• • • • •

Throughout history, women have been told in so many ways what we can and cannot do. But that never stopped women like Harriet Tubman, an escaped slave who became a conductor on the Underground Railroad, leading more than sixty slaves to freedom before the Civil War. It didn't stop Florence Nightingale, who was influential in changing the perception of the nursing profession. It most certainly did not stop Mother Teresa, who devoted her life to serving the poor. Because of her devotion to serving others, Mother Teresa became an icon of service.

And today, there is Greta Thunberg, a young lady who is a global leader for environmental issues, and Nikole Hannah-Jones, a Pulitzer Prize-winning reporter and creator of the landmark 1619 Project. Because of their dedication and purpose, these women have shown us how a legacy is created.

I'm asking you: Who is your hero, and what do you have in common?

Kathy, 63, married, two adult children, real estate agent

What legacy will you leave for your family?

I have not given much thought to my legacy, outside of leaving money to our children.

What other significant things would you like to leave others?

I would like to leave something tangible.

Tell me a little more.

I would like to leave a program for families who don't qualify for a home loan. I would help them get into safe, affordable housing.

If you could create a program, what kind of services would your program offer?

I would offer education on home ownership and the process of buying a home. Our program would provide mentors to guide each prospective home buyer into saving money and getting out of debt.

For someone who did not immediately see her legacy outside of money, you came up with an incredible legacy idea.

I have thought about this for years, and it never occurred to me to act on it. I was too afraid my vision would fail. Now you're causing me to think. When I was in fifth grade, I loved to read, and the library was too far from our house. A teacher from my school named Mr. Taylor drove what he called the bookmobile. It was a big van filled with every kind of book. The bookmobile allowed all the kids in my neighborhood to read and check out any books we wanted. Getting books from Mr. Taylor was the best part of my week. I would be first in line and would always take four or five books to read. I told Mr. Taylor I wanted to be just like him one day. He just smiled. Mr. Taylor's legacy was giving of his time to ensure the children in the neighborhood continued to read throughout the summer months. If I can do a fraction of the good Mr. Taylor did for us, I would be incredibly happy. I am inspired to get my legacy started!

Who inspired you?

• • • • •

Annabel, 49, single, teacher

I wish my parents had thought about a positive legacy for their children. Instead, they left my siblings and me with a legacy of fighting and bickering constantly. Our parents would fight day in and day out. As kids, we knew nothing else. My parents never came to open house throughout my childhood, and they did not help with homework. I don't know if they just wouldn't help or they couldn't help. As a child, I promised myself I would not be in that type of relationship, just being miserable and wasting my life. Because of my parents, I decided to become a teacher.

The legacy that I want to leave behind is a legacy of education. I don't plan to win the Nobel Peace Prize for my efforts; however, I want to make a difference in the world. Every day, I see students struggle in school for various reasons. Parents are not always able to help their children with their homework. Many parents are working long hours or two jobs to make ends meet. There are times when parents do not cooperate with me as the teacher, and I do my best to meet parents where they are currently in their life. I would like to create something for girls, perhaps a science center, to get them more involved with science. I feel like I have been given this talent for a reason, and if I fail to do something, I'm part of the problem and not the solution.

In each interview on legacy, the women did not focus on the legacy they would be leaving; they were living the legacy each day. Women believe their voice is a legacy to their daughters. Mothers today want to ensure their daughters are seen and heard in the 21st century. That they won't be afraid to stand out in a room or be silent and 'go along to get along.' It is okay to cause disruption.

• • • • •

Chapter 8: Friends
and Frenemies

True friends extend encouragement and promote
your right to be you.
— Pamela Hardy-Shepard

• • • • •

Dawn, 49, married, event planner and Leslie, 52, married, banker

Dawn's number was given to me by a friend of mine. I had called her to introduce myself and find out the best time to conduct the interview. During the call, Dawn's best friend, Leslie, was visiting. I could hear bits and pieces of a conversation between the two of them.

Leslie said, "I want to be involved. I heard about this event called Sip and Something, and I couldn't make it."

I asked if they both wanted to speak to me now, that it would only take about thirty minutes. They both talked among themselves and agreed.

What is friendship to you? Who taught you about friendship? Either one of you can go first.

Dawn: I don't think anyone taught me about being a friend, but I watched the friends that my mother had, and the friends adored her. My mother's friends would call the house, and she would talk on the phone and then later go shopping with them. She would come back home with a new outfit and make plans for another shopping venture for the next couple of weeks. My mother and my dad had friends that our entire family would visit, like the Dooley family. My parents would play Pokeno, and my brother and I would play with their two sons and daughter. I really did not think about who taught me about friendship. I guess if I had to answer, it would be my parents. I would say that having a friend is like having an angel on your shoulder.

It's like the bible says, one who has unreliable friends soon comes to ruin, but there is a friend who sticks closer than a brother. And that's my friend Leslie. I've known Leslie for more than twenty-five years. We both have had ups and downs in our lives. Leslie has been there when my own family was not there for me. Let me tell you about this woman. She has so much wisdom. I don't know where it comes from, but she used to say, 'Life is a journey, and on this journey, you will climb hills and fall into valleys. It will rain on you, or even snow. But no matter what, you will go through it by facing the hills, valleys, the rain, or snow one bit at a time.'

There were so many days when bad things happened to me. I didn't want to get out of bed, but because of the encouragement from Leslie, I got up and walked through what seemed to me to be fire!

Leslie: Wait a minute, I wasn't the one who was always the positive one. There was that time when I didn't get that promotion, and it went to that man with less experience. I was angry and hurt. I didn't think I could go back to work the next week, but I went back with a chip on my shoulder. I complained day in and day out. It was Dawn who said, 'I know you're hurt, and it seems unfair, and it is. But you cannot stay in this place of pity. You have to let it go. That job was not for you. There is something better for you that has your name all over it! If you will be patient and let God give you what is meant for you, you will see that your work is not in vain. I promise you.'

If you know anything about Dawn, she does not make false promises. I listened and sucked up my feelings and decided to let my anger go. I realized that I was hurting myself more than my boss's decision not to promote me. Six months went by, and the guy that was promoted was fired. The supervisor took his work and split it among five other employees, including me. I was happy then that I hadn't gotten the job, because I could see what was expected for the job duties. I knew at that moment that job was not for me, and neither was the company. Through another colleague of mine, a huge opportunity appeared, and I took it! If it hadn't been for Dawn saying what she said to me, I might have missed an amazing opportunity.

It sounds as though a true friend tells you the truth whether you want to hear the truth or not. A real friend lifts you up when you're down.

Dawn: You are exactly right, Pamela! Our friendship is built on trust and love. We accept everything about each other, including the things we don't like. We've never tried to change each other. We only show each other another option, and we make our own decision to change or not. We've seen the good, bad, and the ugly side of each other, and still we are friends! We're genuinely happy for each other for our successes as we grow and mature. We have kept each other's secrets, no matter what. We are comfortable around each other, and we both know things about the other that no one will ever know.

Listening to both of you, your friendship also sounds like a marriage. A true friendship has some of the same elements as a marriage. You two have an authentic friendship, one that cheers each other on and is there when you reach a new pinnacle in your life! It sounds as though you two are genuine friends.

Leslie: Many times, my husband has asked me, 'Who are you married to?' He doesn't always understand our friendship, and I don't try to make him understand. There are things I would never say to my husband that I say to my best friend! Men are wired so differently.

Dawn: My husband told me, 'I'm not one of your girlfriends. I don't want to know all of that stuff you guys talk about.' When I stopped telling him things, I think he noticed but never said a thing. I no longer looked for him to share girlfriend stuff. Most of the time, he never understood what I was talking about in the first place, or he would give me some logical response. What I started to do was to share headlines from the news. As women, we need to be supported by our best friends or friends. It is in our DNA.

How do you two remain friends this long?

Dawn: We simply let each other be themselves. Would you agree, Leslie?

Leslie: Yes, not only be us, but become our best selves! We both know life is short and friendship is important.

Have either one of you lost friendships in your life? (Both replied yes.)

Could you both give me an idea of how this happened?

Dawn: People change. What initially brought you together as friends may not be enough to sustain the relationship going forward.

Leslie: Time and chance happen to us all. Life happens, and it waits on no one. Over time, people mature and see their world differently. Basically, you outgrow some people in your life. When this happens, I don't see it as a bad thing. Think back to how they made your life better and be grateful.

I thanked Dawn and Leslie for their time and insight. I believe that people enter our lives to give a lesson, get a lesson, or both. Life does not guarantee the length of stay for anyone in your life. It could be a day, month, or years. Whatever time you are given, be grateful for the time and move on.

• • • • •

April, 45, single, biologist

My mother told me that having friends is like having a diamond. Some diamonds shine more brilliantly than others. Some diamonds will have few flaws, and others have many. She asked me. 'What type of diamond would you want to have as a friend? A diamond that has a yellow cast and many flaws or one that is brilliant with minor flaws?"

I said, 'I want the brilliant diamond with minor flaws.'

She said, 'Remember that the most brilliant diamond with less flaws must be cleaned often to ensure it maintains its brilliant shine and sparkle.'

I thought I'd picked the right answer, but somehow, I don't think I did. My mother didn't tell me the correct answer, so I paid attention to big diamonds, small diamonds, brilliant and not so brilliant diamonds. I finally figured it out. A diamond is a diamond, and they all have a price. Throughout the years, I have come to believe that friends are like diamonds. Some friends sparkle like a princess cut diamond, and the cost in time is more than I can afford. Friendship takes time, so be careful who you label as your friend. It could be that the person is an associate that you spend some time with, but they are not your friend. Associates are people that you don't let in your business. Associates will smile to your face, and some will carry your information onto their friends or associate. Before you know it, everyone knows your man is cheating or your life is in financial ruin. Someone who betrays you is never a friend, and not everyone should gain access to your business.

How do you know when someone is your friend?

My friends are loyal to me, as I am to them. We keep each other's secrets, and we don't share information about the other. When I'm down or they're down, we're there for each other.

I thought I had a friend once. She was a kind person, smart and funny—a princess cut diamond. We both had similar values and enjoyed some of the same things. But one day, I noticed that she would often dismiss the goals I shared with her. On one occasion, I told her about my weight loss goal. Instead of being happy for me, she said mean things. When I lost a pound or two, she said things like, 'You can't even see you lost two pounds. Maybe when you lose twenty pounds.'

At first, I dismissed what she said as me being too sensitive. Until the day I had finally lost twenty pounds. She did not say a word, nor did she celebrate with me on achieving my goal. On another occasion, we went shopping, and she told me that I was too big for this certain outfit, although we were the same size. When I introduced her to my other friends, she would always upstage my friends or tell information about me to prove she knew me longer or we were the best of friends. When I met her friends, I was happy to meet them and didn't try to be the center of attention or tell stories that only she and I knew.

I eventually stopped calling, and she did as well. Our friendship became a cordial hello. If we met in public, we both would speak. I could no longer put my energy into a friendship that was no longer authentic.

Is there anything else you wish your mother could have told you about friendship?

I wish my mother had told me more about her friends and what she learned from her mother. Learning from others is easy when you're looking from the outside in. I think mothers should spend more time with their daughters, making sure their daughters have great self-esteem to become successful, well-rounded women. One more thing, our mothers cannot teach us everything. They can only provide the information that they know. There is a responsibility for women to seek out knowledge and understanding from others, such as their friends. It is my hope you select friends who want to see you succeed.

I thanked April for her insight on friendship and frenemies. Friendship is something you prioritize in your life. We give time to people or things we value.

· · · · ·

Alexa, 54, engaged, project manager

Before we can start discussing friendship, we better start with how to be a friend to the end. You need to look at yourself. When I say look at yourself, consider who you are as a would-be friend and what you bring to the friendship. My question to women is, 'Why would someone want to be friends with you?' Knowing some basic information about yourself is key. What are my values in life? What are the things that I need to change in my life? How am I perceived by others?

Think about this: If you were at your own funeral, what would people say? I had a good friend who told me, 'Look at your circle of five friends, and you will be able to calculate your income by those five people in your circle.' I say that your circle can tell who you are as a person. Your friends are like a mirror, reflecting your character and deeds each day. If you do not like the reflection, change it!

I am intrigued by your comment. Who taught you these things?

Men taught me!

Men taught you this?

Yes! It was not any of the women in my life, not my mother, grandmother, or aunts. It was being in relationships with men. I really have some incredible men in my life. Every male friend has always been loving and, most importantly, honest and encouraging. The men in my life know who they are, and their knowledge was demonstrated in their values. I learned from each of them. As I look back on my life, each one encouraged me to excel and cheered me on to accomplish whatever I set my mind to. As my circle began to grow, often men would say one thing while my female friends in my life said something completely different.

Can you provide an example?

Sure. As a little girl, I was fascinated by architecture and wanted to get my degree in architecture. I always had this desire to see the world. I wanted to see places like the Leaning Tower of Pisa, the Roman Colosseum, the Pyramids of Giza, the Louvre Museum, and the Terracotta Warriors. My male friends would encourage me to go and experience these famous landmarks in the world and learn about the architecture and culture in each place. My female friends would ask me questions like, 'Why do you need to go to these places? You don't know anyone.' And then one of my friends said, 'You have everything you need right here.'

Those two would go on and on about how something bad might happen to me. The remarks were totally different from my male friends, who would tell me to pursue my dreams. My girlfriends would bring me down about my dreams. I finally stopped telling my girlfriends about travel, education, or my goals. It always felt like the two of them were in competition with me.

My male friends would say. 'Those two are not your friends.' At first, I didn't listen or understand. I couldn't get my head around why my two friends would be so negative to me. Both women are accomplished, have great paying jobs, and are beautiful! Today, my good friends are males. Please don't get me wrong. There are some women I get along with, but I don't have a female best friend. I guess the bottom line is this: pick your friends well. Know that your friends make a big difference in your life. If your friends do not respect you and treat you well, let them go.

I thanked Alexa for her time, knowledge, and insight. Friendship is an important part of life.

Be sure who you value values you!

• • • • •

Chapter 9: Mind, Body and Spirit

I have been on a journey to find that sweet spot called balance. As women, we struggle to create a delicate balance between mind, body, and spirit amidst all the other things we do. I can say for sure that there will never be an exact balance. Still, I will prioritize the things I value most. It is difficult to give equal time to everything in your life. Some things will garner more time and attention than others. We must be compassionate with ourselves as we navigate this thing called life. I hope the following stories will inspire you as you read how these women created tried and true ways to balance their lives.

• • • • •

Susan, 45, married

Can you please tell me how you created balance in your life?

As a woman, I feel it's difficult to have balance in my life. Thinking back, I didn't consider having balance as something important. When I was in my thirties, I was having fun partying and doing everything you do when you're young. It caught up with me.

I started looking at my skin, and I felt like I looked old because of my partying, drinking, and smoking a pack of cigarettes a day. Right then, I knew I needed to change. I asked my friend Cara, who is spiritually sound and a longtime vegan, for help. Cara is a sweet woman who never judged me for my lame life decisions. She would bring me vegan food to try, and I would throw it away once she left my house; I was mean. I'm glad to say I am not that person anymore, but it took years for me to change my life.

What prompted your change? What did you do?

I was having a breakdown, and I was going off the rails when Cara reached out to me. She gave me love and support. She introduced me to some of her friends and encouraged me to seek help. She explained to me that seeking help was not a negative thing. So, I did. I met with a counselor for fifteen months. I learned that I could ask for help and not be ashamed. I began to understand that I had a purpose in life other than sex, drugs, and rock 'n' roll. I learned the importance of faith to get me through. I started reading everything I could get my hands on—one of my favorite books is *Return to Love* by Marianne Williamson. I learned about how things in my life will change when I change my mindset. I also read several books by Dr. Wayne Dyer; my favorite is *The Power of Intention*. Between the books and friends, these things helped me to see that I am worth living a great life, a life where my body and mind are healthy and a life where I am in tune spiritually.

What advice would you give to help other women?

Everyone who meets me knows that I will tell the truth about where I have been in life. I can talk about my life and let other women who are facing difficult times in their lives know that there is a better day coming. I would simply say, it will get better; hang in there. We all need some encouragement from time to time. If I can change my life for the best, they can change their lives too. In the movie *The Shawshank Redemption*, Andy Dufresne said, 'Get busy living or get busy dying.' I would rather live a life of passion and help other women see who they can become.

Susan's insight was powerful. It does not matter where we have been; it matters where we are going. We can get busy living or get busy dying. Our life is right now; there are no do-overs. The choices we make today have a culminating effect on the circumstances of our life.

Your circumstances can be turned around for good. Choose well.

• • • • •

Emma, 52, divorced, product manager

You have an interesting journey to health. Could you tell me a little about how you got started on your journey with health and wellness?

I was a mess. My whole life was a mess. I was in a bad relationship. I was out of shape, overweight, and had diabetes.

Each day I went to work seeing other women who looked like they had it all together. I often wondered how they kept it together. They looked good and seemed healthy and happy. I would listen to their stories each morning when I visited the breakroom for coffee and hear different conversations about what was going on in their lives. Their lives sounded nothing like mine. From the outside, everything looked good. I would hear about where they traveled, shopped, or concerts they attended. My weekend was spent just getting through until Monday. Most people are waiting for the weekend. I couldn't wait for Monday so I could escape my weekend of war with my husband.

I buried myself in my work so I wouldn't have to think about my problems at home. I didn't work out or even try to eat healthily. I would eat at McDonald's for lunch, just walking by the cafeteria with a great selection of food. I was so overwhelmed I just didn't know where to start.

It must have been one of those days. I was in the elevator, and I started talking to a woman in there with me. One conversation led to another. We met for lunch the following day in the cafeteria. Kim bought a chef's salad, fruit, and water. I picked up pepperoni pizza and a diet coke. We found a table and sat down, and we began to eat our lunch. I immediately asked Kim, 'Are you on a diet?'

She said, 'No, this is how I eat. I want to be healthy.'

I said, 'I want to be healthy too, but I just can't get started. Look at me. I'm fat and have diabetes!'

Kim said, 'I am looking at you, and I see a beautiful woman. If you don't like what you see, what are you willing to do to change it?'

In my head, I said, Whoa, no one has ever said anything like that to me before. Out loud, I said, 'I would do anything to change the way I look and feel.'

Kim said, 'Why don't we do this together? I would love the company, and we can be each other's accountability partner.'

I agreed, and we started the next day. Usually, each morning I would go into the breakroom to get a coffee and a donut to start my day. Kim changed her break time and met me in the breakroom. I was about to get my usual donut and coffee when Kim walks into the breakroom. She smiled, and I understood her smile. She never said a word. Instead, she offered me some green tea and fruit. I thanked her, and we both went to our offices.

We met every day without fail. I started working out, and in the first three months, I lost fifteen pounds. I felt better. My attitude changed, and I felt happier than I had for years. My husband even noticed the change in me and asked, 'What have you been doing?' I must admit that I played dumb at first and said, 'What do you mean?'

He said, 'You look different.'

I look different, really? I just thanked him and quickly changed the subject.

Why didn't you share your great news?

I didn't want to share with him at the time because of the way he treated me in the past. He wouldn't spend time with me because I was overweight, so my thoughts were he can just continue his behavior like before. Why change now? Seven months later, I lost a total of forty-five pounds. I began reading labels, and I joined a plant-based club at my job. I didn't become a vegan, but I reduced the amount of meat I ate each week.

Did you share with your husband what you were doing?

No, I divorced him. We were not happy for a long time, and the change in me caused a change in him. His attitude became much worse, and I said enough. I'm much happier now. I have peace in my life. Everything isn't perfect, but I now enjoy every weekend come rain or shine!

What was the change in you?

When I gained some success with my weight loss, I became more confident in my abilities. I felt good about myself. I can even say I liked myself. I started shopping for new outfits, cut my hair, and bought new makeup. I remember I used to pull and tug on my clothes to make sure I was hiding my body. Now when I get up in the morning, I feel like I can fly. I have less weight to carry around, and I have so much more energy. I have one regret;

I wish I had done this sooner. If I knew then what I know now, I could have been living my best life sooner.

Do you believe when something is meant for you, it will show up?

Yes, I do. I just wish it had shown up earlier...*(She laughs)*

I thanked Emma for sharing her journey and being transparent. Change comes when the person is ready and not one minute sooner.

What change would you like to see in your life?

• • • • •

Chapter 10: Change Happens When You Are Not Looking

Writing this chapter, I was reminded of my why for writing this book. I wondered why some women successfully navigate their lives, whereas other women's lives were filled with disappointment and despair. When I started this journey, I quickly discovered most of the women's life experiences were different. Nevertheless, each woman used their experiences, good or bad, to grow. They used their power and skills to change the world from where they stood. The book became a call to action, and the stories remind us of our individual and collective power as women.

The stories from the interviews, the survey, and the Sip & Gab focus group produced several overarching themes that could not be ignored. There was a clear, concise demonstration of women's power, whether women embraced their power or not. Women advised readers to own their power, and each interview brought a light of transparency. Additionally, some of the women interviewed had incredible 'aha' moments while discovering their worthiness to receive true love, abundant health, a successful career, a loving family, and a meaningful legacy. A paradigm shift had happened to these women, and the thoughts and expectations of others no longer dictated happiness and fulfillment.

Someone once shared with me an adage that sticks with me to this day: 'I think it, I say it, and I do it.' Our thoughts are powerful. Whatever we believe to be the truth will be so in thought, word, and deed. One negative thought begets another and another, and it is easy to find yourself in a hole and wonder how you got there.

It is essential to share your story to help empower others. You must share life's possibilities, noting you were not always where you are today. Describe your path to faith and success while giving others hope. This book is a reminder to ask for help, too, when we need it and without shame.

I hope these stories have inspired you as they have me. I have gained unwavering respect for each woman in this book—and in the world— and their ability to endure sorrow, hold on to the possibility of love, and garner the power of purpose.

Your bright light does not diminish mine!

Things to ponder:

How can you change your circumstances?

How can you shift in your thinking?

How can you become intentional?

How can you pay it forward through encouragement?

How can you lift as you climb?

Your sister's keeper.

• • • • •

Survey: A CONVERSATION WITH WOMEN

A conversation with women was another way to learn more about women's lives. Women were sent an invitation to participate in the survey and to provide their thoughts to questions at their leisure. The information gathered provided a deeper understanding of how women leaned into womanhood, love, sex, friendships, relationships, menopause, and regrets. The respondents provided additional knowledge that aligned with the responses from the one-on-one interviews and the Sip & Gab event. I found the responses to be informative and transparent.

Q1 Womanhood: Please tell me, where did you get your sense of being a woman? Did you receive your knowledge from your mother, grandmother, friends, or society? Please elaborate.

R1: From my mother and grandmother.

R2: My sense of being a woman came from my mother. As I have grown, my friends have been a more significant influencer on what it means to be a woman.

R3: My grandmother. She was such a strong woman. She would work in the grape fields to keep a roof and food in our mouths. Her faith was strong. She cared about her clothes and her beauty. Grandmother would have conversations just about life.

R4: My mother was the primary role model and a good one. I was also raised Roman Catholic, so we discussed Mary as the mother of Jesus Christ. I was also coming of age during the rise of feminism and during a time when women were more supported in church ministry.

R5: I got my womanhood from my mother, grandmother, and watching the other women in my family. Looking and experiencing their lives raising children and being in relationships.

R6: All the above.

R7: From my mother and grandmother. They were both healthy and faith-driven. These women faced some severe trials in life and overcame them.

R8: Mother.

R9: My mother, aunts, and older cousins.

R10: Mother.

R11: Mother.

R12: Friends. My father raised me without a positive female role model. My circle of friends nurtured me and sparked my sense of femininity and womanhood.

R13: I received most of my information about motherhood by watching other women. My mother, sister-in-law, and first cousin, who had kids very young, were crucial influencers. I wish I had the opportunity to learn from my grandmothers. From the stories I was told, they are significantly different, but both had interesting lives. Since my mother grew up without a mother, it shaped how she mothered her children. There were gaps in her knowledge, but she did her very best to show us the love she never received.

R14: Back in the 50s, girls wore skirts. Society has a strong influence. From my mom, I had a lesson on how not to be a mother, so beginning in 1963, when my son was born, I found my way while I was a U.C. Berkley student. Role models were Gloria Steinem, Jane Fonda, Marianne Williamson.

R15: It is hard to pinpoint. It may have been my first encounter when I was first involved in an intimate relationship with my first serious boyfriend. Other than that, I had no knowledge from any of the adult women in my life.

Q2 Beauty: Now that you are a more mature woman, do you still believe you are beautiful? If so, please tell me why? If not, please tell me what it would take to make you be/feel beautiful?

R1: Not as much as I did when I was younger.

R2: Now, in my life, I do believe that I am beautiful. The younger version of myself did not feel like I was beautiful or enough.

R3: I feel more beautiful now than I did when I was younger. I have accepted what I thought were flaws are not. I love being a more mature woman.

R4; Yes! Although I still would like to lose a few pounds, my leading beauty and what I see as beautiful is a vibrance about life—good energy, laughter, and positive outlook!

R5: I believe I'm a beautiful woman because of my soul and love of God and others.

R6: I believe I'm still beautiful but realize that often when I walk into a room, I'm invisible to many men.

R7: I now believe I'm beautiful. More so from the inside out. As a woman of color, I felt because of my full lips and broad nose, I wasn't beautiful. Having curves and no breasts, I felt inadequate to other women. Now that I am older, I appreciate my attributes.

R8: Respondent skipped question.

R9: Yes, I still believe that I am beautiful.

R10: A tummy tuck.

R11: Beauty is in the eyes of the beholder. I was beautiful the day I was born, and I am still beautiful in and out. Beauty isn't on the outside of one's body. It starts from within. I feel there are several kinds of beauty. I feel beautiful and don't go looking for it.

R12: I just turned fifty and feel more radiant than ever. Ironically, I notice at the same time I'm becoming more invisible to society, but that doesn't deter from my sense of inner beauty.

R13: Mindfulness and emotional intelligence make me beautiful and balanced in a body that needs to be more fit and energetic.

R14: Yes, I feel I'm beautiful as I embrace my new body, wrinkles, and everything else that comes with aging. There are improvements that I would like to make, but I'm not trying to be my twenty-year-old self. I'm also trying to age gracefully. So, I keep my wardrobe fresh, eat well and occasionally exercise to maintain a healthy weight.

R15: I do believe I'm beautiful, for I am fearfully and wonderfully made. That does not mean I don't have times of doubt, as Satan is always on the attack, and there are insecurities for women who have not had a strong relationship with their earthly father. When I keep my focus on my Heavenly Father, I am strong in who He has created me to be.

Q3 Regrets: Do you have any regrets in your life? If so, what are they? What would you do differently? If you do not have any regrets, please say why. What advice would you provide to a younger woman about regrets?

R1: That I did not stand up for myself.

R2: I look at life as a series of opportunities to grow and expand. It is hard to look at regrets, because then I would not have evolved into the woman I am today. My advice to younger women is always to be true to yourself and follow your heart and intuition.

R3: My regrets in life are allowing others' opinions of me to affect me. My advice to younger women is to be you and embrace your beauty and flaws, and if you like it, that's all that matters.

R4: Regrets. There are things I would have done differently with 20/20 hindsight, but not what I would consider angst-provoking regrets. God uses all our mistakes for our good if we turn to him.

R5: Any regret I have would be that I wasn't told that it was okay to fail. I would tell a younger woman that we regret the most the things we didn't do.

R6: Regrets I have is not having a family earlier and focusing so much on my career. I would have been opened to love earlier and taken more chances versus playing it safe.

R7: I'm ready for marriage now. I have not been married before.

R8: Respondent skipped question.

R9: Yes, I regret not realizing my worth at a younger age. I regret not working harder at my goals. I also regret not loving myself enough to take better care of me.

R10: Everyone has regrets. If they say otherwise, they are not being truthful with themselves or anyone else.

R11: Respondent skipped question.

R12: I would take better care of my wellbeing, not stress so much about things that never come to fruition, take more time for r and r, trips with friends, and explore the world more.

R13: I was very young, nineteen. At that age, I was not ready because I had no clue who I was. Therefore, I chose my mate blindly, not knowing what I wanted in a mate for life.

R14: I left behind my relationships with men that did not work out rather than compromise and stick it out. Regrets? Only about loaning money as a mistake to friends who dropped me when they could not repay. Advice? Know you're on a journey to your destination, and don't get sucked into a relationship that diminishes you.

R15. My regret is choosing the wrong man to marry while also not regretting who I married because of the son God blessed me with. I regret not having deep conversations with my children about relationships, as I did not feel capable because of the choices I made. Regrets can help open the door for conversations that can bring healing and forgiveness when they are confessed to those you feel you have hurt by your lack of wisdom and understanding. Although there are some things I wish I had done differently, I view regrets as necessary experiences that made me who I am today. I would tell a younger woman that she's free to do, feel, and experience life as she chooses. Those choices are yours to own, and only yours. Don't allow others to choose your experiences for you.

Q4 Marriage: Were you ready to get married? Did you go into the marriage with a good idea of what to expect? How do you keep your marriage fresh?

R1: Too young. I thought it would be pie in the sky.

R2: I was married at a very young age of twenty-one, and that marriage did not work out. I'm in my second marriage of twenty-seven years, and it was an excellent idea. My husband and I are best friends, and that is the most important thing. We have been able to stick together and support each other through many challenges in our lives.

R3: Yes. I was ready to get married. I went into marriage with a good idea of what to expect. I had to get rid of some baggage I brought with me. We travel a lot, and we have to tell each other when we need to have a date night.

R4: I got married at age thirty-three, and I was ready. I had been serious about getting married for several years. I think I had a perfect idea of what to expect. My parents stayed together through difficult circumstances and always loved each other through it all. And I had a sense of what I did not want. I keep my marriage positive by making a conscious effort to feel gratitude toward my husband.

R5: I am a widow and have been for seven years. I dated before I healed, so I continued making the same mistakes repeatedly.

R6: I'm no longer married. I probably wasn't ready the first time. I am not sure if anyone knows what to expect, because each relationship/marriage is unique.

R7: I am single. Dating is hard. It's hard to meet men who are transparent, willing to be vulnerable and honest. I remain hopeful.

R8: Respondent skipped question.

R9: I was incredibly young, nineteen. At that age, I was not ready because I had no clue who I was; therefore, I chose my mate blindly. Not knowing what I wanted in a mate or life.

R10: Not married.

R11: No. I wasn't, but I'm glad I did. Never go into marriage with high expectations.

R12: I was not ready for marriage, although I had been with my partner for eight years before we married. I had very few examples of healthy marriage or relationships in my life. It just seemed like the thing to do because everyone else thought so. We stayed married for twelve years. In the last ten, we were mostly platonic. We did not keep it fresh.

R13: Married for twenty-two months and nine months, so I claim to be single. Dating has been an adventure in self-discovery and emotional intelligence as a way to save me from compromise.

R14: I felt I was ready at the time. It's a journey, and I'm learning more each day.

R15: My intentions for marriage were self-centered. I rushed with my decision because I wanted to be married and thought I found the right person. However, I was not aware of how to make the best choice. Also, I should have focused on being the right person for marriage. I passed up some good guys because of my lack of wisdom in this area. My focus now is trying to be who God wants me to be, but it is still a struggle. I'm happiest when I am focused on Him. I struggle when I do not.

Q5 Mothers: What things do you wish your mother told you? What things did your mother tell you that changed your life for the best?

R1: Put me first, instead of everyone else.

R: I wish my mother had been supportive of me and my choices.

R3: Nothing.

R4: My mother always conveyed love and acceptance with a listening ear. I can't think of what I would have wished for differently.

R5: Respondent skipped question.

R6: I wish my mother had told me more about her mother. She always encouraged me to do my best.

R7: Respondent skipped question

R8: I wish she could have been able to teach me how to be a good wife to my husband. My mother told me to be independent, to learn how to do things for myself. Also, that no one owes me anything.

R9: Respondent skipped question.

R10: To use birth control.

R11: Respondent skipped question.

R12: My mother left when I was five and was not an influence in my life.

R13: No memory to answer this.

R14: I've learned (and am still learning) to love unconditionally, which also changed my expectations. It is not an easy thing to do, because it is challenging to accept someone fully. One thing I would change is how I communicate. I would try to be more open about my feelings.

R15: I wish she had taught me about life and been more engaged in my well-being. I had a difficult life growing up that caused me to doubt my self-worth until I encountered a loving God that shows me my value every day if I let Him. My mom did not tell me anything that changed my life, but she showed me that through the hardships she faced, she was always working hard to take care of her three daughters with limited help from my father.

Q6 Love: Is your love relationship all that you expected? Please share what you would change or keep the same?

R1: Yes and no. I would change me.

R2: My love relationship is expanding every day, as I am more willing to be more heart-centered.

R3: No. I wish he were more affectionate.

R4: My husband is not my romanticized perfect man I might have wished for before I met him. He loves me and will sacrifice for me. We are good companions, and we like spending time together. I'd love to have a more friendly and outgoing partner with familiar friends, but that is not him. I'm fortunate to have a wonderful man who loves me and loves God, and I value and love.

R5: I'm not in a love relationship.

R6: My love relationship is not what I expected. But I am hopeful in the future it will be. I would remain honest about what I want and have no false expectations.

R7: Respondent skipped question.

R8: Respondent skipped question.

R9: I am married. Relax and enjoy. Never stop working on your relationship.

R10: No love here. I have a sugar daddy.

R11: Respondent skipped question.

R12: My current relationship is passionate, which can be useful and evil. We both love and fight fiercely. Very different from my marriage. The only change I would make is practicing more non-violent communication.

R13: All my love relationships have been a compromise, short, and forgettable.

R14: I've learned (and am still learning) to love unconditionally, which also changed my expectations. It is not an easy thing to do because it is difficult to accept someone fully, flaws, etc. One thing I would change is how I communicate. I would try to be more open about my feelings.

R15: I am back in a relationship with a previous boyfriend that I was engaged to almost thirty years ago. Love is difficult when it's selfish. I have learned to speak up for what's important to me, and I'm willing to walk away if I'm not equally yoked spiritually. I have learned that if I place God first in my life, then every relationship I have will be better for it, because God is teaching me to love others unconditionally. I still have a lot of work to do in this area, and I know it will be a journey throughout my life.

Q8 Sex: Are you single or married? What advice would you provide to a younger woman about sexual relationships?

R1: Don't give yourself away.

R2: Married. It is crucial that you make decisions about your sexual relationships and don't get pressured by outside people.

R3: Married. Save yourself for marriage, so you will not have any extramarital experiences to compare with your mate.

R4: Married. I wish I had gotten hormones earlier to enjoy sex more often when my husband wanted more of it. Now that I have them, I am more easily aroused, but as an older man, he has ED-type problems.

R5: I would say that it is true that a woman's body and her sex is a gift. Make sure the person has proven to be worthy.

R6: I am single. I would tell my daughter not to rush into a sexual relationship as it often makes it more challenging to discover if it is a relationship that could last.

R7: No, not really. But I'm hopeful that in the future it will be. Be honest about what I want and no false expectations.

R8: Respondent skipped question.

R9: Never stop dating and working on your relationship.

R10: Don't do it.

R11: Respondent skipped question.

R12: Regarding sex, I would tell younger women to allow themselves to experience and receive pleasure. To achieve this, I would encourage them to find partners they can trust and feel safe exploring. Sex is not a shameful experience, but a powerful one that can connect us more greatly with ourselves and our feminine powers.

R13: Use protection to postpone conception until you are ready for being a mother.

R14: Married. Choose wisely and be patient. Know your body better than your partner. Treat your body as a temple. It's your choice, not his.

R15: Wait to have sex until you are married. It's not worth having that intimate relationship if it is not with the man you will grow old with. Guard your heart and find other ways to fulfill that longing in your heart. Also, to focus on becoming the woman God wants you to become. Additionally, it's important to link up with a mature woman of faith to help you in this journey.

Q9 Friendships: Please tell me about your friendships. Has the quality of your friendships changed over time? What would you tell a younger woman about friendships? How important are your friends?

R1: They change over time.

R2: I have lost several close friendships to death, which is very sad. My friendships have always been significant to me.

R3: The advice I give to young women is, befriend yourself first and then be friends with others. I also tell them not everyone is your friend. Choose wisely.

R4: Friends are excellent listeners, but they have others in their lives.

R5: My relationships have more significant expectations. I now want positive, honest people to pour into me.

R6: I have always been blessed with good friends. When I was divorcing, my grandmother sent me a poem with a line I always remembered. 'Love may come, and love may go, but friends are the sunshine of life.' My friends are incredibly important to me. I'm loyal to them, and they are loyal to me. They are my own created extended family. I would tell a young woman to create friendships and nourish them all her life.

R7: It's not about the number of friends but the quality of them. I don't have friends from my childhood, but I have some from college. Appreciate and value the different stages a friendship goes through. You grow together, and it's a lifetime commitment. I have a trustworthy six or eight friends that are my ride and die till the wheels come off.

R8: Respondent skipped question

R9: You only get a few real friends in life. Cherish them. Be a good friend. You don't have to have many friends, sometimes just a few close ones at a time.

R10: I have deep, long-lasting relationships.

R11: Respondent skipped this question

R12: Friends are critical in our understanding of ourselves. They are our mirrors, our reflections, our sounding boards, and our safe spaces. I would encourage young women to hold each other up, find sisterhood, and nurture it.

R13: Many friends, both genders. Some from fifty and sixty years ago.

R14: I've had a core set of friends for thirty-plus years. We accept and admire each other, and we still visit one another and travel together. I miss a few childhood friends, but I'm happy that I found my lifetime friends. They are like family to me. I would tell a younger woman to accept friends for who they are and know that everyone has flaws.

R15: I used to need to be accepted by my peers, so I don't feel like I was who I was, but what I thought I should be. Now I'm more content with fewer, more meaningful relationships, and I'm content even if I'm home alone. I also fulfill my need for relationships with like-minded friends who are focused on living a life in obedience to God. I try to be a true and faithful friend so that God will bless me with true and faithful friends.

Q10 Menopause: Please tell me what you were told about menopause. Were you given information from a doctor, friend, sibling, or mother? What would you tell another woman about menopause?

R1: Nothing, I had to find out on my own.

R2: I was given information from my doctor because I was trying to get pregnant, and I was in early menopause.

R3: I embraced menopause. Menopause for women is different. I experience no hot flashes and try to control my attitude. I would tell another woman it is different for each woman.

R4: Not given much info about menopause. I'd tell other women to consider bioidentical hormone replacement for emotional and physical vitality.

R5: Respondent skipped question.

R6: I heard and read so many things about menopause. It's hard to sort out who gave me what information. I would tell another woman having severe symptoms to seek out a doctor who does not knee-jerk about not using hormones.

R7: Not applicable.

R8. Respondent skipped question.

R9: Not much information. Take care of yourself. I'm just starting the journey. Leading up to menopause was stressful, emotional, and exhausting. I had to do a lot of self-help. I changed things in my life that were causing me stress.

R10: Unsure.

R11. Respondent skipped this question.

R12. Most of what I have heard is how horrible it can be. My belief is it is a necessary phase and requires nurturing and going within. While I'm not yet experiencing symptoms of it, I plan to receive them with self-love. I would offer the same advice to other women.

R13. Book called *Hot Flashes*.

R14. I wasn't told much at all. Although most of my girlfriends are menopausal, we seem to suffer in silence. My doctor tested me, asked a few questions, and confirmed it. That was the extent of the conversation. One girlfriend invited me to a conference where I received more information than before. I would tell another woman to embrace the change and seek out information (conference, doctor, or friend) to know what to expect. And then share that information with her daughter.

R15. I just heard all the jokes. I didn't know anything until I went through it. Once I was experiencing it, I had a good OB/GYN that provided information. Still, no one told me of natural ways to counteract the hormone shift, only to take hormones.

Our experiences as women are so different, and yet we have many similarities. I thanked each woman who participated in the survey and spoke their truth as they knew it. Several common themes arose from the survey: It is essential to know ourselves as women and love ourselves and our bodies before entering a love relationship or having sex. Having close friends matters in our lives as women. Picking the right man to be our life partner is necessary to have a fulfilling life.

• • • • •

Sip & Gab Focus Group

The Sip & Gab Event during the holidays provided another opportunity for women to share their thoughts. Several women were invited to participate and were asked to invite at least one other person to the event. As a result, a diverse group of women came together to eat a little food, drink a little wine, and talk about sex.

Women shared face-to-face with strangers, and by the end of the night, the participants had become friends. This dynamic group of women left nothing unsaid when it came to sex and being a woman; they were all in. I am grateful for their time and transparency.

• • • • •

Sex and How We See It

Do you believe that there are two kinds of women, those who want power in the world and those who want power in the bed? What are your thoughts?

Lexi: My sex starts here, in my brain. And it's how you behave and what you say and how you act. Right. I mean, is that how you guys think?

Pat: I agree. Men say we are all emotional. My head says one thing while my heart says, I need the whole thing! I need to know that you care about me. I want to hear the words, and I want to know he is emotionally connected to me because that makes it so much more for me than being alone.

April: I agree. I cannot put my heart in one section and my body in another. Men seem to compartmentalize love and sex.

Paula: In this world, I want to leave my mark. I'm talented and passionate about things. Being passionate is how I feel about my power. It's by doing as much as possible in my life, including my Day Care business. I'm changing children's lives, so that's my power for the world. Sexually, I make sure my partner is happy, and their needs are met as well as mine in the bed.

Tia: Take the power from the bedroom, I don't like the idea of power. I don't want to have power. I want to have influence, which does the same kind of thing. Power just has a different connotation in my mind. So, I want to use the power or the influence to help my friends, family, and partners see sex through a different lens. So, I'm kind of in a space where I'm trying to have sexual influence outside the bedroom.

Marci: That makes sense. Are you saying sexual like a woman walks through the door into a room and has an aura that radiates throughout the room, and everyone in the room is saying, Wow, she's amazing. That kind of sexual influence on other people?

Tia: Not exactly, you see, I'm super open-minded, and I talk to all my friends about sex. So, I want to help people figure out their sexual freedom. I talk about my own experience and use it to help free their mind.

How do you know that their mind is not already free?

Tia: Based on how they use sex as a tool to get what they want.

Lexi: As women, we have to step into our power and own it. We don't have to be ashamed of our sexuality in any way.

Pat: For me, I like to say both power in the world and power in the bedroom. I want to be able to leave a mark on the world as well. In the bedroom, I want power over my sexuality to do what I want without inhibitions.

April: Hmmm…I want power in the bed, but I had minimal power in the bedroom early on in my life. I thought being married meant we were to serve each other's needs. Sad to say, I was never pleased during our sexual encounters. I was there for his sexual pleasure. What I know now is that he was selfish and terrible in bed.

Tia: Wow, so I get it.

Paula: I want to be a change agent. I want to make an impact, and I want to make a difference. That's why I worked so hard on my business and all those other things—I always see a bigger picture in my mind. I want to have a strong influence on young kids, and that's why I continue to get my education. So, power in the world. But then when I think about the power in the bedroom, how do you define power in the bedroom?

What do you think power in the bedroom looks like for you?

Lexi: I think power in the bedroom can be defined as liking yourself just the way you are.

Paula: And so, for me, it's not necessarily to dominate my partner, but for me to be confident in who I am and confident in my sexuality and not having shame about how I look. I think appearance has always been one of those things for me throughout my life, what with my fluctuation of weight. And so being comfortable in my expression is where I see the power in the bedroom. So, it's unnecessary to have power over my partner, but I want to have the strength to stand in who I am as a woman and feel good about being a woman and expressing myself sexually. And that expression of who I am shines out in other places. It's not necessarily in a sexual manner, but it's just standing in my power, if that makes sense?

Tia: Yes, it makes a lot of sense. When you feel comfortable in your skin and look, it is a win.

Pat: As women get older, they think, Oh Lord, things are starting to go South. How do I keep this intact? How can I feel comfortable in the new skin I'm in?

April: I think you have to be grateful where you are, but it is easy for me to say now because I'm not fifty or sixty years old.

Paula: This is a general statement. Most young women don't think about things like power in the world or power in the bedroom unless taught. I didn't know about things like a dry vagina or drooping breasts, either! The problem is that NO one is talking about these issues with younger women. We have to find out on our own.

Marci: Men have such confidence. They can go to the restroom in front of you, and it seems as though they don't care. They swing that thing around and do whatever they do. And they have such confidence in their bodies. A man can be out of shape and not that handsome, and still think he is hot shit! But I think as women, we have been socialized to have some shame. Look around—men can get old, and they are distinguished. Women get old, they are old. Have you ever seen women around a table? We fold in. Men spread out that same confidence that in the meeting room seems to permeate the bedroom. Women have so much power, and we don't even know it. Men will kill for what we have between our legs. They will even go to war over it.

Paula: When I was in my twenties, I had no concept, not until recently.

Marci: There is a book called *Momma Gina's Womanly Arts*. In the book, the author talks about the pussy's power. But I think most women are not aware their pussy has power, not a clue. It is about passing that knowledge down.

Tia: Older women, they don't necessarily tell you that you have this power. Not at all. Maybe it's because they don't know they have power, or they had the power, but now it is gone. You can be confident in whatever you want, but I believe that older women failed younger women. Some older women did not tell us about power and sex because they had not been taught. You can see it in their faces, that 'Don't talk about sex' look. I know that we do not equip young ladies who are coming into their late teens, early twenties. Let me see. We don't get the information from our mothers, church, or older women, so where does that leave us? With magazines, movies, or the guy you think loves you?

Do you talk to younger women?

Tia: Do I talk to them? Yes, the younger women I know, I speak with them. However, there is still a disconnect.

Marci: My mother did not want me to have sex early, but she said this to me, and it shocked me. She said, 'If you are going to have sex, you make sure you get your orgasm.' My mom talked to me; she told us all about sex. Then she said, 'When you are ready to have sex, talk to me.' She was all about birth control. You can be on birth control all day, but if you don't know what you are doing when the penis enters your body—and most young ladies don't—then you are looking for a big disappointment. But nobody ever talks about that or an orgasm. I think for most mothers, it's an embarrassing topic.

So how do you help your daughter or younger women explore their bodies? How do you teach them about what is pleasurable to them? If a woman does not know what she likes, how will she communicate that to her man?

Marci: When guys are young, they do a lot of fumbling around, doing whatever, not experienced at all. It's like society or some people make it taboo to self-pleasure for women.

Pat: I figured it out in my twenties or a little after that. I said to my best friend, 'Come on, girl, let's go. Let's go to the store and get our toys!' Unfortunately, we don't talk about things like that either. My mother did not talk to me about sex toys, I think mostly because she didn't know herself.

Marci: When I read Mamma Gina, she said, 'Hold a mirror down there.' I don't know a lot of women who've ever even looked. I should be looking at my stuff, with a mirror and a flashlight, looking at every nook and cranny?

I was like, huh. The author challenged me to look at every aspect of my pleasure palace.

Lexi: My mother did not tell me to look, either. I would look at the top, but to get a mirror and a flashlight? That is different. It was eye-opening to me, but I think it gave me the knowledge to know how I look, and if something changed, I would know.

Paula: I think it is essential for young ladies to live on their own. When we were young, we were not encouraged to live on our own. Unfortunately, I didn't take the opportunity myself. And I kind of wish I did, because maybe I could have learned some of the things that I know now. I'm still learning about the effects of not learning about my sexual life because I was looking for things, like love, I should have looked for in other places.

What would you have learned about sex by living by yourself?

Lexi: I would have learned early on the importance of responsibility and that having sex was not being in love. I ended up with three kids and three baby daddies! I did not believe in myself and what I had to offer. I'm still here and by myself and struggling every day. So, I think it is crucial to believe in yourself. I don't regret failing to believe in myself, though, because I don't regret my kids.

What would you tell a younger woman? What do you want her to know?

Marci: I would tell her to first love herself and her body. It's more important than looking for somebody else to value you. Learn to be by yourself. Be your cheerleader. There will be those times when someone will treat you disrespectfully, and you will have to speak up and tell them, 'Excuse me, this is not how you treat me.' Once you speak up for yourself, you will not have any regrets. You stood up for yourself. It may make the person who disrespected you do two things: change or leave.

Paula: Exactly. I wish I knew what I know now. I wish I had read books or talked to others. At that time, I didn't know there was another way of being, like valuing myself. And because of it, I made mistakes and had to deal with the negative impact of those mistakes. Those mistakes showed up as having kids too early.

Tia: I don't have kids, but I had something else happen to me. It made me who I am today, and I would not have learned so many other things if it wasn't for that. So it's interesting. I don't have any real regret. I wish that I had learned more when I was younger.

Could you share what you learned?

Lexi: Sure, I learned that trust alone is not enough. You must trust and verify your sex partner has a condom on, or you know they have a clean bill of health that is documented, or no cookie.

Pat: I could not agree more!

Marci: I'm going to use that: trust, and verify.

Pat: I believe that a person's background experience, economic knowledge, and what they are exposed to will put a woman on a path of what she may become.

Marci: That is so true. Yeah, the things you mentioned offer awareness and education. I worked at a job where we created Empowerment Sessions, bringing women together to talk about important topics. In doing so, we exposed women to dialogue and discussions to help empower and educate at the same time. So, I think it would be more of a grassroots effort to expose women who would otherwise be isolated.

Tia: As a teacher, we can see what is being taught in the home. It is our job to teach reading, writing, and arithmetic, though, and not teach other concepts that should be taught at home. We cannot cross that line.

Marci: I teach the girls to speak up for themselves. That's how I sneak it in.

Tia: I love that you tell young girls to speak up, because when I was a little girl, no one did that for me. I didn't want to speak up when I was inappropriately touched. I knew it was wrong, but there was no one there for me. I thought no one would believe me. There was no one I trusted to tell. We must communicate to girls and boys that if someone touches you in your private place to speak up.

Marci: That's right. Talking about it helps young girls to know they have a voice and that they can speak up, instead of just being passive about it. We must help young girls to be more assertive. So, women must learn to speak up as well as listen. Everyone needs to listen. One of the problems is that we're always formulating our answers as people speak. We don't listen to one another. I want to give you my answer, and that's what I want to do.

• • • • •

Regrets That Changed My Life

I'm going to shift here for a moment and ask you, are there any regrets that you have, something that maybe you would have changed, or would have liked to have done differently? How would that play out today? Such as sexually, physically, spiritually, or relationship-wise? What are the big standouts for you?

Pat: I would have changed the communication in my family, because I wasn't told anything. So, I learned everything on my own.

April: Ha…What I learned, I learned on the street. I wish my parents had been more open. I couldn't go to my mother and ask her what a blow job was. I figured she wouldn't know what it was anyway. So, I wished I could have talked to my mother about things I wanted to know.

Pat: Sad to say, our parents did not discuss these things. It's like, you know how when your parents tell you about sex and some parents try to use the birds, bees, and animals, to explain two people having sex. That's what sex is, birds having sex? Where is the love in this example?

Lexi: The regret I think most children have with their parents is when they tried to talk about sex with them, they put sex in one box and love in another. And then you get in relationships, and you don't know what is what. It's sad.

Marci: I have no regrets about sex. When we were young, my mom and dad would bring us all together in their room and talk about sex. At school, the bathroom door opened, and I saw a boy. I thought he was peeing on the wall. So I could ask those kinds of questions. It could be about where do babies come from. My brother and me could ask questions, and if my cousins were there, they would get the lesson too. They would teach us all. So, I remember the mini-lessons, and I'm grateful for them. They did not discuss anything like a blow job, though.

April: There's this New Age kind of spiritual stuff that's coming out. I see it on Instagram, and there are podcasts. So there's a sex coach or sex therapist. One lady speaks about her daughter, and she talks about how she talks to her daughter and all that kind of information. So, I'm hoping that maybe that's a new change, and that people will start talking about sex more in a beautiful way.

Pat: Economic status, background experience, all those things are part of what people are exposed to as they are growing up.

Tia: That is so true.

Maria: One of my biggest regrets is that I married the wrong man at a young age, and it haunted me for a while.

Pat: My biggest regret is that I got pregnant at eighteen and did not have a plan in my life.

Lexi: I wish my mother had taught me how to be an advocate for my self-care. I've gotten older, and I wish I knew earlier what I know now.

Pat: I think if I had known that I am somebody of value, my life would have been different. I take what has happened to me in life and use it to my best of ability.

I want to thank each woman who participated in the interviews, survey, and the Sip & Gab. The women presented in this book may or may not represent your story as a woman. However, you can indeed find a woman's story that you know. Each voice provided solidarity, support, and encouragement to the reader. No matter what obstacles the women faced in this book, they overcame their obstacles through love and friendship.

• • • • •